ID0440983

07-CFZ-880

Lexical Aids for Students of
New Testament Greek

Bruce M. Metzger, Ph.D., D.D.

Professor of New Testament Language and Literature
Princeton Theological Seminary

ENLARGED EDITION

Published by the Author
Princeton, N. J.
1957

PHOTOLITHOPRINTED BY CUSHING - MALLOY, INC.
ANN ARBOR, MICHIGAN, UNITED STATES OF AMERICA
1957

οὐ πόλλ' ἀλλὰ πολύ   'not quantity but quality'

(literally, 'not many things but much')

μελέτη τὸ πᾶν   'practice makes perfect'

(literally, 'practice [is] everything')

PREFACE

According to the psychologist, man learns by associating the new with the old, the strange with the familiar. In studying a foreign language, therefore, the beginner will do well to observe whatever similarities may exist between his own and the other language.

Part I of the following *Lexical Aids* makes use of this principle of associative learning by supplying, after the English definitions of Greek words, such English derivatives as may be of assistance in remembering the meaning of the Greek vocabulary. The Greek words in the list, furthermore, have been selected and arranged in accord with their frequency in the New Testament.

Part II makes a different application of the same psychological principle. Here are exhibited the family relationships among words of frequent and less frequent occurrence. After a student has become acquainted with a minimum working vocabulary of words which occur many times in the New Testament he can make more rapid progress in acquiring a larger vocabulary by learning such additional words as resemble in general meaning and form those which he already knows.

What proportion of attention should be devoted to Part I ('Words Classified according to Their Frequency') before beginning to employ at the same time Part II ('Words Classified according to Their Root') can be determined on the basis of economy of time and effort. A judicious and faithful use of both Parts will speed the day when the beginner can read the Greek Testament with pleasure and profit.

The author wishes to express his deep gratitude to four graduate students at Princeton Theological Seminary for their assistance in proofreading the typescript. They are Mr. Irvin W. Batdorf, Teaching Fellow in New Testament; Mr. Willard A. Beling, Teaching Fellow in Old Testament; Mr. Henry Voogd, Teaching Fellow in Old Testament; and Mr. Lawrence E. Yates, formerly Student Assistant in New Testament Greek at Presbyterian College, Montreal.

October 1, 1946

Preface to the Enlarged Edition

At the time of the sixth printing of this little book, it is appropriate to accede to the requests of some who have used it in the classroom that future printings include a list of the principal parts of verbs which occur most frequently in the New Testament. Accordingly, Appendix IV has been added to this enlarged edition. Furthermore, in order to provide assistance in another area of New Testament lexicography, a list is given in Appendix V of all the nouns of the second declension which end in -ος and which are feminine in gender.

Perhaps it may be confessed here that the Greek couplet which stands at the foot of the last page is doubly appropriate -- no less for the compiler than for the user of this booklet. This colophon, with which many a weary scribe in the Middle Ages brought his manuscript to a close, may be rendered, 'As strangers rejoice to see their native land, so also is the end of a book to those who labor!'

BRUCE M. METZGER

December 16, 1954

CONTENTS

Words Classified according to their Frequency

According to J. H. Thayer's *Greek-English Lexicon of the New Testament* (p. xviii), the Greek New Testament makes use of 5594 different words. More than one half of these occur only once, twice, or thrice. Of the remainder, nearly eleven hundred appear in the New Testament ten times or more. All of these, with the exception of proper names,[1] are included in the following word list and are arranged in descending order of their frequency.

The usefulness of such a list is obvious. By consulting it the beginner will not, so to speak, waste his time memorizing words which occur only rarely in the New Testament. He can be assured that when he has learned, say, the first 510 words of the list he then knows *all* of the words (other than the proper names) which occur at least 25 times in the New Testament.

The beginner of any foreign language always finds it easier to acquire a working knowledge of the vocabulary if he is shown parallels between it and his own language. Though several grammars for beginners of Classical Greek are provided with such mnemonic aids (as, for example, the grammars by H. L. Crosby and J. N. Schaeffer, and by A. S. Way), grammarians of New Testament Greek have been slow in adopting this pedagogically sound procedure. As a start in this direction there

[1] As a rule the proper names in the Greek New Testament so closely resemble the corresponding names in English as to occasion very little difficulty of recognition. A table of equivalent letters in transliteration is given below on pages 3 f.

1

have been added to the following frequency word list such English derivatives as seemed likely to prove helpful to the student of New Testament Greek. It need scarcely be mentioned that not every Greek word has an English derivative. Nevertheless, a surprisingly large proportion of the following words can be supplied with more or less well-known English derivatives.[2] The derivative, which is italicized and enclosed within parentheses, is not to be confused with the definition of the Greek word. The definition is to be memorized; the derivative is intended to be of assistance in remembering the definition. Although many other examples of English derivations from these Greek words might have been cited, those which are given were chosen with an eye to the probable interests of the type of student who will make use of this list. That is, whenever it was possible to do so, derivatives were provided which involve theological, ecclesiastical, or patristic terminology.

In some instances the derivative is not direct but is from a closely related word in Greek. In these cases the English word is introduced by the abbreviation 'cf.' (='compare'). Thus, for example, the definition of the noun διδάσκαλος is followed by '(cf. *didactic*),' for, although no noun in English is a direct derivative of διδάσκαλος, the adjective *didactic*, being derived from a closely related Greek word (διδακτικός), will serve as a mnemonic aid in remembering the meaning of διδάσκαλος. In a few instances, when not even this sort of indirect derivative is available in English, a cognate word is cited. Thus, after the definition of πατήρ one finds '(akin to *paternal*),' for *paternal* closely resembles πατήρ because the English word is derived from the Latin *pater* which

---

[2] To be exact, 447 of the 1055 words which occur ten times or more are provided with English derivatives. This is about 42 per cent.

in turn is a cognate of the Greek word.[3]

Attention may be called to the occasional use of a word or phrase enclosed within parentheses in conjunction with the definition of a Greek word. Thus, ἀποστέλλω is defined '*I send* (with a commission).' The words within parentheses will not be confused with the English derivative, for the latter is in every case printed in italics. Again, it will be observed that a semi-colon is used (1) to separate quite diverse English definitions of the same Greek word, and (2) to separate two or more English derivatives from one another.

The following table of equivalent letters and diphthongs will be of assistance in learning to become aware of many English derivatives other than those which are cited by way of example. The Greek letters whose transliteration is immediately obvious are not included.

CONSONANTS

Greek	English	Examples
γγ	ng	εὐαγγέλιον, *evangel*
ζ	z	ζωή, *Zoe*
κ	c (sometimes k)[4]	ἐκκλησία, *ecclesiastic* κινέω, *kinetic* εἰκών, *icon* (also *ikon*)
ξ	x	ξύλον, *xyl*ophone
φ	ph	φωνή, *-phone*
χ	ch	εὐχαριστία, *Eucharist*
ψ	ps	ψεύδομαι, *pseudo-*

[3] For further information regarding cognate words, see Appendix I.

[4] In general when a Greek word has entered English through Latin it has c for kappa; when it has come direct, it has *k*.

VOWELS AND DIPHTHONGS

Greek	English	Examples
η	e	ζωή, Zoe
(initial) ι (followed by a vowel)	j	ἰῶτα, jot
		Ἰησοῦς, Jesus
υ	y	ψυχή, psyche
αι	e (or ae)	αἷμα, hemoglobin (or haemo-)
ει	i (or ei)	εἰκών, icon
		δείκνυμι, deictic
ευ	eu, before a vowel, ev	εὐ + φημί, euphemism
		εὐαγγέλιον, evangel
οι	e (or oe)	οἰκουμενικός, ecumenical
		(also oecumenical)
ου	u	οὐ + τόπος, Utopia
(final) ια	(frequently) y	εὐλογία, eulogy

A few observations as to the most efficient ways in which to use the following word lists may not be out of place. The usual and time-tested procedure is to concentrate on a Greek word and to repeat it to oneself over and over again with the English definition. In doing so one should be careful always to put the stress on the syllable of the Greek word which carries the accent mark. Otherwise, if, for instance, ἀδελφός be pronounced *a'del-fos* today, and *a-del'fos* tomorrow, and *a-del-fos'* at another time, the labor of learning the one Greek word is practically tripled.

Likewise of great importance in the proper pronunciation of Greek words is a knowledge of the rules governing their division into syllables. These principles are simple. There are as many syllables in a Greek word as separate vowels or diphthongs. (1) A single consonant standing between two vowels in

one word belongs with the second vowel, as ἀ-γά-πη. (2) A group
of consonants that can begin a word (which may be seen from a
lexicon), and a group formed by a consonant followed by μ or ν,
belongs with the second vowel. (3) A group of consonants that
cannot begin a word is divided between two syllables, as ἐλπίς, ἀ-μαρ-τά-νω. Doubled consonants are divided, as θά-λασ-σα.
(4) Compound words divide at the point of union, as εἰσ-φέρω,
συν-έχω.

Another exceedingly helpful method of learning a foreign
language is to write the unfamiliar words. Indeed, according
to the author of a popular treatise on the study of languages,
this method ought to be practiced by every one learning a new
language. Frederick Bodmer declares, 'Pen (or pencil) and pa-
per are essential help. We are most apt to forget what we take
in by ear, least likely to forget what we learn by touch. No
one who has learned to swim or cycle forgets the trick of doing
so.'[5] Most students discover that the effort of writing helps
to fix their attention on the task at hand and thus impresses
the new words more firmly in their memory. It is recommended
that, in order to gain the greatest benefit from the word lists,
the student utilize both the oral and the written discipline.
Moreover, in addition to memorizing lists of words, the highest
degree of proficiency in translating the New Testament can be
attained only if long sections of the text be read, preferably
aloud.

In counting the frequency of Greek words in the New Testament, the author has utilized W. F. Moulton and A. S. Geden's
A Concordance to the Greek Testament (2nd ed., Edinburgh,
1899). It may be mentioned that Moulton and Geden's orthography

[5] *The Loom of Language* (New York, 1944), p. 28.

follows that of Westcott and Hort in their edition of the
Greek New Testament.

The definitions have been purposely kept brief and
pointed, yet it is hoped that no denotation which occurs
with any degree of frequency has been neglected. For further
information as to various connotations and nuances of meaning,
the following standard lexicons may be consulted.

Abbott-Smith, G., *A Manual Greek Lexicon of the New Testament*
    (3rd ed., Edinburgh, 1937).

Reasonably complete and not unwieldy, but does not make full use
of new material.

Arndt, William F., and Gingrich, F. Wilbur, *A Greek-English
    Lexicon of the New Testament and Other Early Christian
    Literature*, a translation and adaptation of Walter
    Bauer's *Griechisch-Deutsches Wörterbuch zu den Schriften
    des Neuen Testaments usw.*, 4te Aufl., Berlin, 1949-52
    (Chicago and Cambridge, 1957).

Best of New Testament lexicons, with rich bibliographical data.

Cremer, Hermann, *Biblisch-theologisches Wörterbuch der neu-
    testamentlichen Gräzität* (11th ed., edited by Julius
    Kögel, Gotha, 1923); *Biblico-Theological Lexicon of
    New Testament Greek* (3rd English ed., translated from
    the German of the 2nd ed., with additional matter and
    corrections by the author, Edinburgh, 1880); and *Sup-
    plement to Biblico-Theological Lexicon of New Testament
    Greek* (Edinburgh, 1886).

Though superseded by Kittel, contains much valuable material.

Kittel, Gerhard (ed.), *Theologisches Wörterbuch zum Neuen
    Testament* (Stuttgart, 1933 —).

Combines strict philological accuracy with theological insight;
unparalleled source of information.

Liddell, H. G., and Scott, Robert, *A Greek-English Lexicon*,

    new ed., revised and augmented throughout by H. S.

    Jones, assisted by Robert McKenzie (Oxford, 1925-1940).

  The standard lexicon of classical Greek. The preceding edition (the 8th) is more serviceable for learning the usage of early ecclesiastical writers.

Moulton, J. H., and Milligan, George, *The Vocabulary of the*

    Greek Testament Illustrated from the Papyri and other

    Non-literary Sources (London, 1914-1929; one vol. ed.,

    1930).

  Defines only those words on which the editors found fresh information in the papyri and other non-literary sources; unsurpassed in its field.

Preisigke, Friedrich, *Wörterbuch der griechischen Papyrusur-*

    kunden mit Einschluss der griechischen Inschriften, Auf-

    schriften, Ostraka, Mumienschilder, usw., aus Ägypten

    (Berlin, 1925-1931).

  A general lexicon of the papyri.

Sophocles, E. A., *Greek Lexicon of the Roman and Byzantine*

    Periods (from B.C.146 to A.D.1100) (Memorial ed., New

    York, 1887).

  Old and occasionally disappointing, but the only one-volume lexicon covering the field.

Souter, Alexander, *A Pocket Lexicon to the Greek New Testament*

    (Oxford, 1916).

  Fresh, vivid definitions; its faults are those of extreme brevity and lack of helps for locating forms.

Thayer, J. H., *A Greek-English Lexicon of the New Testament*

    (Corrected ed., New York, 1889).

  For several generations the best general lexicon for the pastor, but now superseded by Arndt and Gingrich's translation of Bauer.

Zorell, Franciscus, *Lexicon Graecum Novi Testamenti* (2nd ed.,

    Paris, 1931).

  A useful Greek to Latin lexicon by a capable Jesuit scholar.

Words Occurring More Than 500 Times

ἄνθρωπος, -ου, ὁ, a man

ἀπό, with the gen., from (apostasy, standing [στῆναι] off from)

αὐτός, -ή, -ό, himself, herself, itself, same; he, she, it
  (auto soterism, the doctrine that man is saved by his own
  efforts or character)

γάρ, for

γίνομαι, I become, am

δέ, but, and

διά, with the gen., through; with the acc., on account of
  (diameter, measure across or through)

ἐγώ, I (ego)

εἰμί, I am

εἶπον, I said (cf. epic)

εἰς, with the acc., into (eisegesis, faulty interpretation of
  a text by reading into it one's own ideas)

ἐκ, ἐξ, with the gen., out of, from (ecstasy, state of being
  [literally, standing, στῆναι] out of one's senses; exodus,
  a going [literally, a way, ὁδός] out)

ἐν, with the dat., in (enthusiast, one possessed or inspired
  by a god [ἔνθεος])

ἐπί, with the gen., over, on, at the time of; with the dat.,
  on the basis of, at; with the acc., on, to, against
  (epidermis, upon the skin [δέρμα])

ἔρχομαι, I come, go

ἔχω, I have, hold

θεός, -οῦ, ὁ, a god, God (theology)

ἵνα, in order that, that

9

καί, and, even , also

κατά, with the gen., down from, against; with the acc., according to, throughout, during (cataclysm, a washing down or against)

κύριος, -ου, ὁ, a lord, the Lord

λέγω, I say, speak (all words ending in -ologue or -ology)

μή, not, lest

ὁ, ἡ, τό, the

ὅς, ἥ, ὅ, who, which

οὗτος, αὕτη, τοῦτο, this; he, her, it

ὅτι, that, because

οὐ, οὐκ, οὐχ, not (utopia, no place [τόπος])

πᾶς, πᾶσα, πᾶν, every, all (Pan-American)

ποιέω, I do, make (poem; pharmacopoeia, making of drugs)

πρός, with the acc., to, towards, with (proselyte, one who has come [root of ἐλθεῖν] to another religion)

σύ, thou

τίς, τί, who? what? which? why?

τις, τι, someone, something, a certain one, a certain thing, anyone, anything

ὡς, as, that, how, about

WORDS OCCURRING 201 TO 500 TIMES

ἅγιος, -α, -ον, holy; plural as a noun, the saints (Hagiographa, the books of the Hebrew Scriptures not included under the Law and the Prophets)

ἀδελφός, -οῦ, ὁ, brother (Philadelphia, [city of] brotherly love [φιλία])

ἀκούω, I hear (acoustics)

ἀλλά, but, except

ἀνήρ, ἀνδρός, ὁ, a man (polyandry, having many husbands)

ἀποκρίνομαι, *I answer*

γῆ, γῆς, ἡ, *the earth* (*geo*politics)

γινώσκω, *I come to know, learn, know, realize*

γυνή, γυναικός, ἡ, *a woman, wife* (miso*gyn*ist, a woman hater [μισέω])

δίδωμι, *I give* (anti*dote*)

δύναμαι, *I am powerful, able* (cf. *dynamite*)

ἐάν, *if*

ἑαυτοῦ, *of himself*

εἰ, *if*

εἶδον, *I saw* (*idea*)

εἷς, μία, ἕν, *one* (heno*theism*, belief in one God without asserting that he is the only God)

ἐκεῖνος, -η, -ο, *that*

ἐξέρχομαι, *I go out*

θέλω, *I will, wish, desire* (**Mono**the*lite*, one who holds that Christ has but one will, the divine; condemned by the Sixth General Council A.D. 680)

ἤ, *or*

ἡμέρα, -ας, ἡ, *a day* (*ephemeral*, for [ἐφ' (=ἐπί)] a day)

λαλέω, *I speak* (cf. *glossolalia*, the gift of speaking in tongues [I Cor. 14])

λαμβάνω, *I take, receive* (epi*lepsy*, a taking or seizing upon)

λόγος, -ου, ὁ, *a word, the Word* (*logic*)

μαθητής, -οῦ, ὁ, *a disciple*

μετά, *with the gen., with;* with the acc., *after* (*meta*physics, beyond or after [Aristotle's treatise on] physics)

οἶδα, *I know*

ὄνομα, -ατος, τό, *a name* (*onomatopoeia*, making [ποιεῖν] a name or word [in imitation of natural sounds], as 'buzz')

οὐδείς, οὐδεμία, οὐδέν, *no one, none, nothing, no*

οὖν, *therefore, then, accordingly*

οὐρανός, -οῦ, ὁ, *heaven* (the planet *Uranus;* the element *ura-nium)*

οὕτως, *thus*

πατήρ, πατρός, ὁ, *father* (akin to *paternal)*

περί, with the gen., *concerning, about;* with the acc., *around* (*perimeter*, measure around)

πιστεύω, *I have faith (in), believe*

πίστις, -εως, ἡ, *faith, belief, trust*

πνεῦμα, -ατος, τό, *a spirit, the Spirit* (*pneumatology*, the doctrine of the Holy Spirit)

πολύς, πολλή, πολύ, *much;* plural, *many* (*polytheism*)

υἱός, -οῦ, ὁ, *a son*

ὑπό, with the gen., *by;* with the acc., *under* (*hypodermic*, under the skin [δέρμα])

WORDS OCCURRING 151 TO 200 TIMES

ἄγγελος, -ου, ὁ, *a messenger, an angel* (*angel*)

ἁμαρτία, -ας, ἡ, *a sin, sin* (*hamartiology*, the doctrine of sin)

ἄν, *an untranslatable word, the effect of which is to make a statement contingent which would otherwise be definite*

βασιλεία, -ας, ἡ, *a kingdom*

γράφω, *I write* (*palaeography*, the study of ancient [παλαιός] writing and manuscripts)

δόξα, -ης, ἡ, *glory* (*doxology*)

ἔθνος, -ους, τό, *a nation;* plural, *the Gentiles* (*ethnology*)

εἰσέρχομαι, *I go or come in or into, enter*

ἔργον, -ου, τό, *work* (*energy*)

ἐσθίω, *I eat* (*anthropophagous*, man-eating [aorist, φαγεῖν])

εὑρίσκω, *I find* (*heuristic*, the method in education by which

a pupil is set to find out things for himself; *eureka*,
'I have found [it], -- *Archimedes*

ἵστημι, *I cause to stand, I stand*

καθώς, *as, even as*

καρδία, -ας, ἡ, *the heart* (cardiac)

κόσμος, -ου, ὁ, *the world* (cosmic, cosmos)

μέγας, μεγάλη, μέγα, *large, great* (megaphone; omega [literally, great 'o'])

μέν, postpositive particle, *on the one hand, indeed* (often it is better left untranslated and its presence shown by stress of the voice and by translating a following δέ by 'but')

νεκρός, -ά, -όν, *dead;* as a noun, *a dead body, a corpse* (necropolis, city of the dead, a cemetery)

νόμος, -ου, ὁ, *a law, the Law* (Deuteronomy, the second [statement of the] law)

ὅστις, ἥτις, ὅτι, *whoever, whichever, whatever*

ὄχλος, -ου, ὁ, *a crowd, multitude* (ochlocracy, mob rule)

παρά, with the gen., *from;* with the dat., *beside, in the presence of;* with the acc., *alongside of* (paragraph, originally, in manuscripts, a stroke or line drawn in the margin *beside* the column of writing to mark the division of sections)

πόλις, -εως, ἡ, *a city* (Neapolis, New City, Acts 16:11; Constantinople, Constantine's City)

πορεύομαι, *I go, proceed*

τε, (an enclitic connective particle, weaker in force than καί) *and*

τότε, *then, at that time*

ὑπέρ, with the gen., *in behalf of;* with the acc., *above* (hypercritical) χάρις, -ιτος, ἡ, grace (Charissa, [girl's name])

χείρ, χειρός, ἡ, a hand (chirography, handwriting)

WORDS OCCURRING 121 TO 150 TIMES

ἀγαπάω, I love

αἰών, -ῶνος, ὁ, an age (aeon)

ἄλλος, -η, -ο, other, another (allegory, description of one
thing under the image of another)

ἀμήν, verily, truly, amen (amen)

ἀποστέλλω, I send (with a commission) (cf. Apostle)

ἀρχιερεύς, -έως, ὁ, chief priest, high priest

ἀφίημι, I let go, permit, forgive (aphesis, the gradual loss
of a short unaccented initial vowel, as 'squire' for
'esquire')

βάλλω, I throw, put (ballistics, the science of the motion of
projectiles)

βλέπω, I see

δοῦλος, -ου, ὁ, a slave

δύο, two (dyad)

ἐγείρω, I raise up

ἕως, until; with the gen., as far as

ζάω, I live

ζωή, -ῆς, ἡ, life (Zoe [girl's name])

καλέω, I call, name, invite

λαός, -οῦ, ὁ, a people (laity)

νῦν, now

ὅταν, whenever

οὐδέ, and not, not even, neither, nor

πάλιν, again (palimpsest, a manuscript which has been used
again, the earlier writing having been erased [ψῆν, to
scrape or erase])

παραδίδωμι, I hand over, betray

προφήτης, -ου, ὁ, a prophet (prophet)

σάρξ, σαρκός, ἡ, flesh (sarcophagus, a [stone] coffin which
    'eats' [φαγεῖν] the contents)

σύν, with the dat., with (syntax, sentence construction, in-
    volving grammatical arrangement [τάσσειν] of words with
    one another)

σῶμα, -ατος, τό, a body (somatic)

φωνή, -ῆς, ἡ, a sound, voice (phonetic)

WORDS OCCURRING 101 TO 120 TIMES

ἀγαθός, -ή, -όν, good (Agatha)

ἀγάπη, -ης, ἡ, love

ἀλήθεια, -ας, ἡ, truth

ἀνίστημι, I cause to rise; I arise

ἀπέρχομαι, I depart

ἀποθνήσκω, I die

βασιλεύς, -έως, ὁ, a king (Basil)

δεῖ, it is necessary

δύναμις, -εως, ἡ, power (dynamite)

ἐκκλησία, -ας, ἡ, a community, congregation, church (ecclesi-
    astic)

ἐξουσία, -ας, ἡ, authority

ζητέω, I seek

θάνατος, -ου, ὁ, death (thanatopsis, a view of, or meditation
    on, death)

ἴδιος, -α, -ον, one's own (idiosyncrasy)

κρίνω, I judge, decide (critic)

μέλλω, I am about to

μένω, I remain

ὁδός, -οῦ, ἡ, a way, road, journey (anode, cathode, electrical
    terminals)

οἶκος, -ου, ὁ, a house (economy, household management)

ὅλος, -η, -ον, whole (holocaust)

ὁράω, I see

ὅσος, -η, -ον, as great as, as many as

ὅτε, when

παρακαλέω, I beseech, exhort, console (Paraclete, the Comforter,
        Helper, Advocate, or Counselor)

πῶς, how?

σώζω, I save (in biochemistry, sozin, any defensive protein
        in the animal body)

ψυχή, -ῆς, ἡ, soul, life, self (all words beginning with
        psycho-)

ὥρα, -ας, ἡ, an hour (horoscope, prediction based on the obser-
        vation of the hour of one's birth)

WORDS OCCURRING 91 TO 100 TIMES

ἀλλήλων, of one another   (parallel, beside [παρ'] one another)

αἷμα, -ατος, τό, blood   (anaemia, without blood; haemoglobin)

αἴρω, I take up, take away

ἄρτος, -ου, ὁ, bread, a loaf

γεννάω, I beget (cf. hydrogen, so called as being considered
        the generator of water [ὕδωρ])

διδάσκω, I teach (cf. didactic)

δικαιοσύνη, -ης, ἡ, righteousness

εἰρήνη, -ης, ἡ, peace (Irene)

ἐκεῖ, there

ἐρῶ, I shall say

ἕτερος, -α, -ον, other, another, different (heterodoxy)

ἕτοιμος, -η, -ον, ready, prepared

θάλασσα, -ης, ἡ, the sea (thalassic)

καλός, -ή, -όν, beautiful, good (kaleidoscope [εἶδος, form, and σκοπεῖν, to behold])

οἰκία, -ας, ἡ, a house

ὀφθαλμός, -οῦ, ὁ, an eye (ophthalmology)

περιπατέω, I walk; I live (peripatetics)

πούς, ποδός, ὁ, a foot (podium)

πρῶτος, -η, -ον, first (all words beginning with proto-)

τέκνον, -ου, τό, a child

τίθημι, I place

τόπος, -ου, ὁ, a place (topography, topic)

φοβέομαι, I fear (cf. phobia)

Words Occurring 81 to 90 Times

ἀκολουθέω, I follow (cf. acolyte, the assistant who carries
the wine and water and the lights at the celebration of
the Mass, following the priest)

ἀναβαίνω, I go up

ἀπόλλυμι, I destroy; middle, I perish (Apollyon, the angel of
the bottomless pit, Rev. 9:11. In Pilgrim's Progress
he appears as a fiend armed with fiery darts whom Chris-
tian overcomes in the Valley of Humiliation)

ἄρχω, I rule; in the New Testament almost always middle, I
begin

ἕκαστος, -η, -ον, each

ἐκβάλλω, I cast out

ἐνώπιον, with the gen., before

ἔτι, still, yet, even

καιρός, -οῦ, ὁ, fitting season, opportunity, time

κάθημαι, I sit

μηδείς, μηδεμία, μηδέν, no one

μήτηρ, μητρός, ἡ, a mother (akin to maternal)

ὅπου, where, whither

πίπτω, *I fall*

πληρόω, *I fill, fulfill*

προσέρχομαι, *I come to*

προσεύχομαι, *I pray*

ὥστε, *so that*

WORDS OCCURRING 71 TO 80 TIMES

αἰτέω, *I ask*

ἀνοίγω, *I open*

ἀποκτείνω, *I kill*

ἀπόστολος, -ου, ὁ, *an Apostle* *(Apostle)*

βαπτίζω, *I baptize* *(baptize)*

δίκαιος, -α, -ον, *right, just, righteous*

δώδεκα, *twelve* *(dodecagon)*

ἐμός, ἐμή, ἐμόν, *my, mine*

ἑπτά, *seven* *(heptagon)*

εὐαγγέλιον, -ου, τό, *the good news* (of the coming of the Messiah), *the Gospel* *(Evangel)*

ἱερόν, -οῦ, τό, *a temple* (cf. *hierarchy*)

καταβαίνω, *I go down*

κεφαλή, -ῆς, ἡ, *head* *(cephalic)*

μᾶλλον, *more, rather*

μαρτυρέω, *I bear witness, testify* (cf. *martyr*)

πέμπω, *I send*

πίνω, *I drink*

πονηρός, -ά, -όν, *evil*

πρόσωπον, -ου, τό, *face* (*prosopography, description of the face or personal appearance*)

πῦρ, πυρός, τό, *fire* *(pyre)*

σημεῖον, -ου, τό, *a sign* (cf. *semaphore*, bearing [φέρειν] a sign)

στόμα, -ατος, τό, *a mouth* *(stomach)*

τηρέω, *I keep*

ὕδωρ, ὕδατος, τό, *water* (*hydrophobia; dropsy* [formerly *hydropsy*])

ὑπάγω, *I depart*

φῶς, φωτός, τό, *light* (*photography*, *writing* [γράφειν] with *light*)

χαίρω, *I rejoice*

WORDS OCCURRING 61 TO 70 TIMES

ἀγαπητός, -ή, -όν, *beloved*

ἄγω, *I lead*

αἰώνιος, -ον, *eternal* (*aeonian*)

ἀπολύω, *I release*

γραμματεύς, -έως, ὁ, *a scribe* (cf. *grammatical*)

δαιμόνιον, -ου, τό, *a demon* (*demon*)

δοκέω, *I think; seem* (*Docetism*, the early heresy that Christ's body was phantasmal or of celestial substance which merely *seemed* human)

ἐντολή, -ῆς, ἡ, *a commandment*

ἔξω, *without;* with the gen., *outside*

θέλημα, -ατος, τό, *will* (*Monothelite*, one who holds that Christ had but one will, the divine; condemned by the Sixth General Council, A.D. 680)

ἱμάτιον, -ου, τό, *a garment*

καρπός, -οῦ, ὁ, *fruit*

κηρύσσω, *I proclaim* (as a herald, κῆρυξ), *preach*

νύξ, νυκτός, ἡ, *night*

ὄρος, ὄρους, τό, *a mountain* (*orology*, the scientific study of mountains)

οὔτε, *neither, nor*

πιστός, -ή, -όν, *faithful, believing*

πλοῖον, -ου, τό, a boat

πρεσβύτερος, -α, -ον, elder (presbyter)

ῥῆμα -ατος, τό, a word (cf. rhetoric)

σάββατον, -ου, τό, the Sabbath (Sabbath)

συνάγω, I gather together (synagogue)

τρεῖς, τρία, three (triad)

φέρω, I carry, bear, lead (Christopher, bearing Christ)

ὧδε, hither, here

WORDS OCCURRING 56 TO 60 TIMES

ἀρχή, -ῆς, ἡ, a beginning (archaic)

ἀσπάζομαι, I greet, salute

δέχομαι, I receive

διδάσκαλος, -ου, ὁ, a teacher (cf. didactic)

δοξάζω, I glorify (cf. doxology)

ἐπερωτάω, I ask, question, demand of

ἐρωτάω, I ask, request, entreat

ἤδη, now, already

θρόνος, -ου, ὁ, a throne (throne)

κράζω, I cry out

λοιπός, -ή, -όν, remaining; as a noun, the rest; as an adverb,
for the rest, henceforth

μέσος, -η, -ον, middle, in the midst (Mesopotamia, in the midst
of the rivers [Tigris and Euphrates])

οὐχί, (strengthened form of οὐ), not

πλείων, -ονος, larger, more

προσκυνέω, I worship

συναγωγή, -ῆς, ἡ, a synagogue (synagogue)

τοιοῦτος, -αύτη, -οῦτον and -οῦτο, such

ὑπάρχω, I am, exist; τὰ ὑπάρχοντα, one's belongings

φημί, I say

χαρά, -ᾶς, ἡ, joy, delight

Words Occurring 50 to 55 Times

ἄχρι, ἄχρις, with the gen., as far as, up to; as a conjunction, until

γλῶσσα, -ης, ἡ, a tongue, language (glossolalia, the gift of speaking [cf. λαλεῖν] in tongues, I Cor. 14)

γραφή, -ῆς, ἡ, a writing, Scripture (Hagiographa, books of the Hebrew Scriptures not included under Law and Prophets)

δεξιός, -ά, -όν, right (opp. left) (akin to dexterous)

διό, wherefore

ἐλπίς, -ίδος, ἡ, hope

ἐπαγγελία, -ας, ἡ, a promise

ἔσχατος, -η, -ον, last (eschatology)

εὐαγγελίζω, I bring good news, preach good tidings (the Gospel) (evangelize)

εὐθύς, straightway, immediately

θεωρέω, I look at, behold (theorem; theory)

λίθος, -ου, ὁ, a stone (monolith; lithograph)

μακάριος, -α, -ον, blessed, happy (macarism, a beatitude)

μηδέ, but not, nor; not even

μόνος, -η, -ον, alone, only (monologue)

ὅπως, in order that, that

παιδίον, -ου, τό, an infant, child

παραβολή, -ῆς, ἡ, a parable (parable)

πείθω, I persuade

σοφία, -ας, ἡ, wisdom (philosophy)

χρόνος, -ου, ὁ, time (chronology)

Words Occurring 46 to 49 Times

ἁμαρτωλός, -όν, sinful; as a noun, a sinner

ἀπαγγέλλω, I announce, report

ἀποδίδωμι, I give back, pay; middle, I sell

ἄρα, then, therefore

ἔμπροσθεν, with the gen., in front of, before

ἔρημος, -ον, solitary, deserted; as a noun, ἡ ἔρημος, the desert, wilderness (hermit)

ἔτος, -ους, τό, a year (the Etesian winds in the Mediterra-
   nean region blow annually)

καθίζω, I seat, sit (cf. cathedral, properly, the church which
   contains the bishop's chair or seat)

κακός, -ή, -όν, bad, evil (cacophony, discord)

κρατέω, I grasp (cf. plutocratic, grasping wealth [πλοῦτος])

κρίσις, -εως, ἡ, judgment (crisis)

μικρός, -ά, -όν, small, little (microscope; omicron, little
   'o')

οὐκέτι, no longer

παραλαμβάνω, I receive

ποῦ, where? whither?

πρό, with the gen., before (prologue)

προσφέρω, I bring to, offer

σπείρω, I sow

σωτηρία, -ας, ἡ, salvation (soteriology)

τρίτος, -η, -ον, third

τυφλός, -ή, -όν, blind (typhlosis, medical term for blindness)

φανερόω, I make manifest

φόβος, -ου, ὁ, fear, terror (phobia)

φυλακή, -ῆς, ἡ, a guard, a prison, a watch

χρεία, -ας, ἡ, a need

WORDS OCCURRING 42 TO 45 TIMES

ἁμαρτάνω, I sin (cf. hamartiology, the doctrine of sin)

ἀνάστασις, -εως, ἡ, resurrection (Anastasia [girl's name])

ἅπας, -ασα, -αν, all

γενεά, -ᾶς, ἡ, a generation (genealogy)

δεύτερος, -α, -ον, second (Deuteronomy, the second [statement of the] law)

δέω, I bind (diadem, literally, something bound around or across)

διώκω, I pursue, persecute

ἐγγίζω, I come near

ἐπιγινώσκω, I come to know, recognize

εὐλογέω, I bless (eulogize)

θαυμάζω, I marvel, wonder at (cf. thaumaturge, a worker of miracles or wonders)

θεραπεύω, I heal (therapeutic)

θηρίον, -ου, τό, a wild beast (theriomorphic, having animal form; as, theriomorphic gods)

θλῖψις, -εως, ἡ, tribulation

κατοικέω, I inhabit, dwell

λύω, I loose (cf. analysis, a resolving or unloosing into simple elements)

μέρος, -ους, τό, a part (in biology, pentamerous, of five parts)

ναός, -οῦ, ὁ, a temple

ὅμοιος, -α, -ον, like (Homoiousian, one holding that Father and Son in the Godhead are of like [but not the same] substance; a Semi-Arian)

σεαυτοῦ, of thyself

σήμερον, today

σπέρμα, -ατος, τό, a seed (sperm)

σταυρόω, I crucify

τιμή, -ῆς, ἡ, honor, price (cf. Timothy, honoring God)

φωνέω, I call (phonetic)

WORDS OCCURRING 38 TO 41 TIMES

ἅπτομαι, I touch

ἄξιος, -α, -ον, worthy (axiom; in philosophy and psychology,
     axiological, pertaining to the science of values)

διέρχομαι, I pass through

δικαιόω, I justify, pronounce righteous

ἐπιθυμία, -ας, ἡ, eager desire, passion

ἐπιτίθημι, I lay upon

ἐργάζομαι, I work (cf. energy)

ἑτοιμάζω, I prepare

εὐχαριστέω, I give thanks (Eucharist)

θύρα, -ας, ἡ, a door

ἱκανός, -ή, -όν, sufficient, able, considerable

καινός, -ή, -όν, new

κλαίω, I weep

λογίζομαι, I account, reckon (cf. logic)

μισέω, I hate (misogynist, a woman hater)

μνημεῖον, -ου, τό, a tomb, monument

οἰκοδομέω, I build, edify

ὀλίγος, -η, -ον, little, few (oligarchy, rule by the few)

οὐαί, woe! alas!

πάντοτε, always

παραγίνομαι, I come, arrive

παρίστημι, I am present, stand by

πάσχω, I suffer

περισσεύω, I abound

πλανάω, I lead astray (planet, to the ancients, an apparently
        'wandering' celestial body)

πράσσω, I do, perform (praxis, practice, as opposed to theory)

πρόβατον, -ου, τό, a sheep

τέλος, -ους, τό, end (teleology, in philosophy, the view that
        developments are due to the purpose or design [end]
        that is served by them)

χωρίς, with the gen., without, apart from

WORDS OCCURRING 34 TO 37 TIMES

ἀγρός, -οῦ, ὁ, a field (akin to agrarian)

ἄρτι, now, just now

ἄρχων, -οντος, ὁ, a ruler (monarch, sole [μόνος] ruler)

ἀσθενέω, I am weak

βλασφημέω, I revile, blaspheme (blaspheme)

βούλομαι, I wish, determine

διάβολος, -ον, slanderous, accusing falsely; as a noun, the Ac-
        cuser, the Devil (diabolical)

διακονέω, I wait upon (especially at table), serve (generally),
        minister (cf. deacon)

ἐκπορεύομαι, I go out

ἐμαυτοῦ, of myself

ἐπιστρέφω, turn to, return

εὐθέως, immediately

καλῶς, well

μαρτυρία, -ας, ἡ, a testimony, evidence (cf. martyrdom)

μάρτυς, -υρος, ὁ, a witness (martyr)

μετανοέω, I repent

ὀπίσω, behind, after; with the gen., behind, after (cf.
        opisthograph, a manuscript written upon both the back

and the front, Rev. 5:1)

ὀργή, -ῆς, ἡ, anger

οὖς, ὠτός, ὁ, an ear (otology)

ὀφείλω, I owe, ought

πέντε, five (Pentateuch)

πειράζω, I test, tempt, attempt

περιτομή, -ῆς, ἡ, circumcision

προσευχή, -ῆς, ἡ, prayer

πτωχός, -ή, -όν, poor; as a noun, a poor man

τέσσαρες, -ων, four (the Diatessaron of Tatian, a harmony of
    the four Gospels made about A.D. 170; literally,
    through [the] four)

ὑποστρέφω, I return

ὑποτάσσω, I subject, put in subjection (in grammar, hypotaxis,
    subordination of clauses)

ὥσπερ, just as, even as

Words Occurring 32 to 33 Times

ἀναγινώσκω, I read

ἀρνέομαι, I deny

βιβλίον, -ου, τό, a book (Bible)

δεικνύω or δείκνυμι, I show (in logic, apodeictic, of clear
    demonstration)

διαθήκη, -ης, ἡ, a covenant

διακονία, -ας, ἡ, waiting at table, (in a wider sense) service,
    ministry (diaconate)

δυνατός, -ή, -όν, powerful, possible (cf. dynamite)

ἐγγύς, near

ἔξεστι, it is lawful

ἐχθρός, -ά, -όν, hating; as a noun, an enemy

ἥλιος, -ου, ὁ, the sun (helium)

26

ἱερεύς, -έως, ὁ, a priest (hierarchy)

καυχάομαι, I boast

μέλος, -ους, τό, a member

μήτε, neither, nor

οἶνος, -ου, ὁ, wine

πλῆθος, -ους, τό, a multitude (cf. plethora)

ποῖος, -α, -ον, what sort of? what?

ποτήριον, -ου, τό, a cup

συνέρχομαι, I come together

ὑπομονή, -ῆς, ἡ, steadfast endurance

φυλάσσω, I guard (cf. prophylactic)

Words Occurring 30 or 31 Times

ἀγοράζω, I buy (cf. agora, the market place)

ἀκάθαρτος, -ον, unclean

ἄνεμος, -ου, ὁ, a wind (anemone; anemometer)

ἀρνίον, -ου, τό, a lamb

γε, indeed, at least, really, even

διάκονος, -ου, ὁ and ἡ, a servant, administrator, deacon
    (deacon)

διδαχή, -ῆς, ἡ, teaching (cf. didactic)

ἐλεέω, I have mercy (cf. eleemosynary; alms)

ἐλπίζω, I hope

ἐπικαλέω, I call, name; middle, I invoke, appeal to

ἐπιτιμάω, I rebuke, warn

καθαρίζω, I cleanse (catharize)

ναί, yea, truly, yes

ὁμοίως, likewise

παραγγέλλω, I command, charge

παρέρχομαι, I pass by, pass away; I arrive

παρρησία, -ας, ἡ, boldness (of speech), confidence

πλήν, *however, but, only;* with the gen., *except*

σκανδαλίζω, *I cause to stumble (scandalize)*

σκότος, -ους, τό, *darkness* (scotoscope, a fieldglass for seeing by night)

συνείδησις, -εως, ἡ, *conscience*

φαίνω, *I shine, appear (phantom; phenomenon)*

φεύγω, *I flee*

φυλή, -ῆς, ἡ, *a tribe* (in zoology, phylum, one of the large fundamental divisions of the animal kingdom)

WORDS OCCURRING 28 OR 29 TIMES

ἀληθινός, -ή, -όν, *true*

γαμέω, *I marry* (in biology, gamete, a matured germ cell)

γνῶσις, -εως, ἡ, *wisdom* (gnosis; Gnostic)

ἐνδύω, *I put on, clothe*

ἐπεί, *when, since*

ἡγέομαι, *I am chief; I think, regard*

θυσία, -ας, ἡ, *a sacrifice*

ἰσχυρός, -ά, -όν, *strong*

κρίμα, -ατος, τό, *judgment* (cf. crisis)

μάχαιρα, -ης, ἡ, *a sword*

μισθός, -οῦ, ὁ, *wages, reward*

μυστήριον, -ου, τό, *a mystery* (mystery)

οὔπω, *not yet*

παράκλησις, -εως, ἡ, *an exhortation, consolation* (cf. Paraclete, the Comforter, Helper, Advocate, or Counselor)

πάσχα, *indeclinable,* τό, *a passover (paschal)*

πλούσιος, -α, -ον, *rich* (cf. plutocratic)

πόθεν, *whence?*

ποτέ, *at some time, once, ever*

προσκαλέομαι *I summon*

προφητεύω, *I prophesy* (cf. *prophet*)

τελέω, *I finish, fulfill* (cf. *teleology*, in philosophy, the
view that developments are due to the purpose
or design [τέλος] that is served by them)

φίλος, -η, -ον, *loving;* as a noun, *a friend* (*bibliophile*)

WORDS OCCURRING 26 OR 27 TIMES

ἁγιάζω, *I sanctify* (cf. *hagiolatry*, the worship of saints)

ἀδελφή, -ῆς, ἡ, *a sister*

ἀδικία, -ας, ἡ, *unrighteousness*

ἀληθής, -ές, *true*

ἀποκαλύπτω, *I reveal* (*apocalypse*)

βαστάζω, *I bear, carry*

ἐκεῖθεν, *thence, from that place*

ἔλεος, -ους, τό, *pity, mercy* (cf. *eleemosynary; alms*)

ἑορτή, -ῆς, ἡ, *a feast*

ἥκω, *I am come*

θυγάτηρ, -τρός, ἡ, *a daughter*

ἰάομαι, *I heal* (cf. *pediatrics*, medical care of children [παῖς,
παιδός])

καταργέω, *I bring to naught, abolish*

κελεύω, *I order*

κώμη, -ης, ἡ, *a village*

λυπέω, *I grieve*

νικάω, *I conquer* (cf. *Nicholas*, victor over the people [λαός])

ὀμνύω or ὄμνυμι, *I swear, take an oath*

πόσος, -η, -ον, *how great? how much?*

σός, σή, σόν, *thy, thine*

σταυρός, -οῦ, ὁ, *a cross*

στρατιώτης, -ου, ὁ, *a soldier*

συνίημι, I *understand*

φρονέω, I *think*

χήρα, -ας, ἡ, a *widow*

χώρα, -ας, ἡ, a *country* (chorography, describing, or description, of districts)

WORDS OCCURRING 25 TIMES

ἀδικέω, I *wrong, do wrong*

ἀναβλέπω, I *look up, receive sight*

γνωρίζω, I *make known*

δέκα, *ten* (Decapolis, the region embracing ten cities mostly SE. of the Lake of Tiberias)

δένδρον, -ου, τό, a *tree* (rhododendron, lit. rose-tree)

δουλεύω, I *serve*

ἕνεκα or ἕνεκεν, with the gen., *on account of*

καθαρός, -ά, -όν, *clean* (catharsis; Catharine)

μανθάνω, I *learn* (mathematics)

μήποτε, *lest perchance*

νεφέλη, -ης, ἡ, a *cloud* (nephelometer)

ὁμολογέω, I *confess, profess*

οὗ, *where*

πνευματικός, -ή, -όν, *spiritual* (pneumatic)

πορνεία, -ας, ἡ, *fornication* (cf. pornography)

προσέχω, I *attend to, give heed to*

φιλέω, I *love* (cf. bibliophile)

WORDS OCCURRING 24 TIMES

ἀκοή, -ῆς, ἡ, *hearing; a report*

ἀναιρέω, I *take up; kill*

ἀσθένεια, -ας, ἡ, *weakness* (neurasthenia, nervous prostration)

ἀσθενής, -ές, *weak* (cf. neurasthenia)

διότι, because

ἐκλεκτός, -ή, -όν, chosen, elect (cf. eclecticism)

ἐπιστολή, -ῆς, ἡ, a letter (epistle)

καταλείπω, I leave

κατηγορέω, I accuse   (cf. categorical)

κεῖμαι, I lie, am laid

νοῦς, νοός, ὁ, the mind (noetic)

παῖς, παιδός, ὁ and ἡ, a boy, girl, child, servant (pedagogue,
          literally, child-leader)

πάρειμι, I am present; I have arrived

παρουσία, -ας, ἡ, presence, coming (especially Christ's
          [second] coming in glory) (Parousia)

περιβάλλω, I put around, clothe

πίμπλημι, I fill

σωτήρ, -ῆρος, ὁ, Saviour   (cf. soteriology)

WORDS OCCURRING 23 TIMES

ἀμπελών, -ῶνος, ὁ, a vineyard

ἀνάγω, I lead up; middle, I put to sea, set sail

ἄπιστος, -ον, unbelieving, faithless

ἀστήρ, -έρος, ὁ, a star (aster)

αὐξάνω, I cause to grow; increase

γρηγορέω, I watch (Gregory)

εἰκών, -όνος, ἡ, an image (icon)

ἐλεύθερος, -α, -ον, free

ζῷον, -ου, τό, a living creature, an animal (zoology)

θυσιαστήριον, -ου, τό, an altar

κοπιάω, I toil

κωλύω, I forbid, hinder

λευκός, -ή, -όν, white (leukemia, literally, white blood
          [αἷμα])

μιμνήσκομαι, I remember (cf. mnemonics)

νέος, -α, -ον, new, young (all words beginning with neo-)

πεινάω, I hunger

πέραν, with the gen., beyond

περισσός, -ή, -όν, excessive, abundant

σκεῦος, -ους, τό, a vessel; plural, goods

τελειόω, I fulfill, make perfect

χαρίζομαι, I give freely, forgive

WORDS OCCURRING 22 TIMES

δέομαι, I beseech

δοκιμάζω, I prove, approve

θεάομαι, I behold (theater)

καθεύδω, I sleep

καθίστημι, I set, constitute

κατεργάζομαι, I work out

κοιλία, -ας, ἡ, the belly (stomach or intestines, or both),
        womb (coeliac, pertaining to the abdomen)

μετάνοια, -ας, ἡ, repentance

μηκέτι, no longer

νυνί, now

πληγή, -ῆς, ἡ, a blow, wound, plague (plague)

πλοῦτος, -ου, ὁ, wealth (plutocrat)

πωλέω, I sell (cf. monopoly)

στρέφω, I turn (strophe)

συνέδριον, -ου, τό, a council, the Sanhedrin (Sanhedrin)

χιλίαρχος, -ου, ὁ, a military tribune, captain (chiliarch)

ὡσεί, as, like, about

WORDS OCCURRING 21 TIMES

ἀγνοέω, I do not know (agnostic)

ἀντί, with the gen., *instead of, for* (all words beginning with
      anti-)

ἀργύριον, -ου, τό, *silver* (in pharmacy, *Argyrol*, the trade-
      name of a silver-protein compound)

βασιλεύω, *I reign*

γένος, -ους, τό, *race, kind* (akin to *genus*)

διδασκαλία, -ας, ἡ, *teaching*

ἑκατοντάρχης (or -αρχος), -ου, ὁ, *a centurion*

ἐκλέγομαι, *I pick out, choose* (*eclectic*)

εὐδοκέω, *I think it good, am well pleased with*

ἐφίστημι, *I stand over, come upon*

θερίζω, *I reap*

λατρεύω, *I serve, worship* (cf. *Mariolatry*)

μνημονεύω, *I remember* (cf. *mnemonics*)

παράπτωμα, -ατος, τό, *a trespass*

πειρασμός, -οῦ, ὁ, *temptation*

τελώνης, -ου, ὁ, *a taxgatherer*

τεσσαράκοντα, indeclinable, *forty*

τιμάω, *I honor* (*Timothy*, honoring God)

ὑπακούω, *I obey*

χιλιάς, -άδος, ἡ, *a thousand* (*chiliasm*, millenarianism)

WORDS OCCURRING 20 TIMES

αἰτία, -ας, ἡ, *a cause, accusation, crime* (*etiology*, the in-
      vestigation of causes)

ἀκροβυστία, -ας, ἡ, *uncircumcision*

βάπτισμα, -ατος, τό, *baptism* (*baptism*)

γονεύς, -έως, ὁ, *a parent* (cf. *gonad*)

ἐνεργέω, *I work, effect* (cf. *energy*)

ἐπίγνωσις, -εως, ἡ, *knowledge*

ἰχθύς, -ύος, ὁ, *a fish* (*ichthyology*)

κρύπτω, *I conceal* (*cryptic*)

μαρτύριον, -ου, τό, a testimony, witness, proof (cf. martyrdom)

ξύλον, -ου, τό, wood, tree (xylophone)

προάγω, I lead forth, go before

σκηνή, -ῆς, ἡ, a tent, tabernacle (scene)

σοφός, -ή, -όν, wise (cf. sophomore, literally, a wise fool
        [μωρός])

ὑπηρέτης, -ου, ὁ, a servant, assistant

ὑψόω, I lift up, exalt (cf. hypsophobia, fear of high places)

WORDS OCCURRING 19 TIMES

ἀπέχω, I have received (payment); I am distant

γεωργός, -οῦ, ὁ, a farmer (George)

διακρίνω, I discriminate; middle, I doubt

δῶρον, -ου, τό, a gift (Theodore, Dorothea [or Dorothy], gift
        of God)

ἐπαίρω, I lift up

ἐπάνω, above; with the gen., over

ἐπιβάλλω, I lay upon

ἐπιλαμβάνομαι, I take hold of

ἐπουράνιος, -ιον, heavenly

ἡγεμών, -όνος, ὁ, a leader, a (Roman) governor (cf. hegemony,
        leadership, especially of one state of a confederacy)

κοινωνία, -ας, ἡ, fellowship; contribution

κρείσσων or κρείττων, -ονος, better

κριτής, -οῦ, ὁ, a judge (critic)

κτίσις, -εως, ἡ, creation, creature

μεριμνάω, I am anxious, distracted

μέχρι or μέχρις, until; with the gen., as far as

νηστεύω, I fast

παλαιός, -ά, -όν, old (palaeography)

παρατίθημι, I set before; middle, I entrust

πότε, when?

προφητεία, -ας, ἡ, a prophecy (prophecy)

τέλειος, -α, -ον, complete, perfect, mature (cf. teleology)

τοσοῦτος, -αύτη, -οῦτο, so great, so much; plural, so many

τρέχω, I run

WORDS OCCURRING 18 TIMES

ἀληθῶς, truly

ἀνάγκη, -ης, ἡ, necessity

ἀποκάλυψις, -εως, ἡ, a revelation (apocalypse)

ἀπώλεια, -ας, ἡ, destruction (cf. Apollyon)

ἀριθμός, -οῦ, ὁ, a number (arithmetic)

βλασφημία, -ας, ἡ, reproach, blasphemy (blasphemy)

δέησις,-εως, ἡ, an entreaty

δεσμός, -οῦ, ὁ, a fetter, bond

ἐλέγχω, I convict, reprove (elenchus, a logical refutation)

ἐμβαίνω, I embark

ἐπιτρέπω, I permit

θυμός, -οῦ, ὁ, wrath

καταγγέλλω, I proclaim

κατακρίνω, I condemn

κατέχω, I hold fast, hold back

κενός, -ή, -όν, empty, vain (cenotaph, sepulchral monument to
          a person whose body is elsewhere)

κληρονομέω, I inherit

κοιμάομαι, I sleep, fall asleep (cemetery, literally, a
          sleeping chamber)

κόπος, -ου, ὁ, labor, trouble

κρυπτός, -ή, -όν, hidden (cryptic)

μήν, μηνός, ὁ, a month (menology, a calendar, especially that
          of the Greek Church, provided with short biographies

of saints)

μήτι, interrogative particle, expecting a negative answer

οἰκοδομή, -ῆς, ἡ, *a building; edification*

προστίθημι, *I add, add to*

παράχρημα, *immediately*

πυλών, -ῶνος, ὁ, *a vestibule, gateway (pylon)*

στέφανος, -ου, ὁ, *a crown (Stephen)*

ταράσσω, *I trouble*

τίκτω, *I give birth to*

ὑποκριτής, -οῦ, ὁ, *a hypocrite*

ὑπομένω, *I tarry; I endure*

φανερός, -ά, -όν, *manifest*

χρύσεος, -α, -ον, contracted χρυσοῦς, -ῆ, -οῦν, *golden (chrys-anthemum, literally, golden flower)*

WORDS OCCURRING 17 TIMES

ἀρέσκω, *I please*

αὑτοῦ, *of himself*

ἄφεσις, -εως, ἡ, *a sending away, remission (aphesis, the gradual loss of a short unaccented vowel at the beginning of a word; as 'squire' for 'esquire')*

βρῶμα, -ατος, τό, *food*

γάμος, -ου, ὁ, *a marriage, wedding (bigamy, double marriage; digamy, second marriage after the decease of the first spouse, condemned as a sin by certain Church Fathers)*

δέσμιος, -ου, ὁ, *a prisoner*

εἰσπορεύομαι, *I enter*

ἑκατόν, *one hundred (hecatomb, great public sacrifice, properly of 100 oxen [βοῦς])*

ἐξίστημι, *I amaze, am amazed*

ἐπαύριον, *on the morrow*

ἐπιμένω, *I continue*

θησαυρός, -οῦ, ὁ, *a storehouse, treasure* (*thesaurus*)

ἵππος, -ου, ὁ, *a horse* (*hippopotamus*, literally, a river-
    horse)

καθάπερ, *even as, as*

καταλύω, *I destroy; I lodge*   (cf. *catalyze*)

κερδαίνω, *I gain*

νίπτω, *I wash*

νυμφίος, -ου, ὁ, *a bridegroom* (akin to *nuptial*)

περιτέμνω, *I circumcize*

πέτρα, -ας, ἡ, *a rock* (*petrify*)

πλήρωμα, -ατος, τό, *fullness* (*pleroma*, in Valentinian Gnosti-
    cism, the world of light, including the body of eons)

πλησίον, **near**; as a noun, *a neighbor*

ποιμήν, -ένος, ὁ, *a shepherd* (*poimenic*, pertaining to pastoral
    theology)

ποταμός, -οῦ, ὁ, *a river* (*hippopotamus*, literally, a river-
    horse)

ῥύομαι, *I rescue, deliver*

σκοτία, -ας, ἡ, *darkness* (*scotoscope*, a fieldglass for seeing
    by night)

χάρισμα, -ατος, τό, *a free* (*gracious*) *gift* (*charism*, a special
    spiritual gift or power divinely conferred; I Cor.
    12)

ὡσαύτως, *likewise*

WORDS OCCURRING 16 TIMES

ἀνακρίνω, *I examine*

ἀπάγω, *I lead away*

δεῖπνον, -ου, τό, *a supper*

δηνάριον, -ου, τό, a denarius (denarius)

διαλογίζομαι, I debate

διατάσσω, I command

διψάω, I thirst (cf. dipsomania, a craving for alcohol)

ἐκτείνω, I stretch forth

ἐκχέω, I pour out

ἐντέλλομαι, I command

ἔπειτα, then

ἐπιθυμέω, I desire

ἐργάτης, -ου, ὁ, a workman (cf. energy)

εὐλογία, -ας, ἡ, a blessing (eulogy)

ζῆλος, -ου, ὁ, zeal, jealousy (zeal)

θεμέλιος, -ου, ὁ, a foundation

κακῶς, badly, ill

κατέρχομαι, I come down, go down

κλείω, I shut

κλέπτης, -ου, ὁ, a thief (kleptomaniac)

πάθημα, -ατος, τό, suffering (cf. pathological; apathy)

παρέχω, I offer, afford

πλήρης, -ες, full

πόλεμος, -ου, ὁ, a war (polemics)

πολλάκις, often

προσδοκάω, I wait for

ῥαββεί or ῥαββί, indeclinable, ὁ, (my) master (rabbi)

ῥίζα, -ης, ἡ, a root (rhizome)

συκῆ, -ῆς, ἡ, a fig tree (sycophant, a flatterer, literally,
          a fig-shower [the reason for the name is not defi-
          nitely known])

συλλαμβάνω, I take, conceive

συνίστημι or συνιστάνω, transitive tenses, I commend; intransi-
          tive tenses, I stand with, consist

σφραγίς, -ἴδος, ἡ, a seal (sphragistics, the science of seals, their history, age, distinctions, etc.)

τέρας, -ατος, τό, a wonder

τολμάω, I dare

τροφή, -ῆς, ἡ, food (cf. atrophy, wasting due to malnutrition)

ὑστερέω, I lack

χορτάζω, I eat to the full, am satisfied, am filled

ὦ, O!

WORDS OCCURRING 15 TIMES

ἀνέχομαι, I endure

γεύομαι, I taste

γνωστός, -ή, -όν, known

γυμνός, -ή, -όν, naked (gymnasium)

δέρω, I beat

διαμαρτύρομαι, I testify solemnly

ἐλαία, -ας, ἡ, an olive tree

ἐπαγγέλλομαι, I promise

εὐσέβεια, -ας, ἡ, piety, godliness (Eusebius)

εὐχαριστία, -ας, ἡ, thanksgiving (Eucharist)

καταλαμβάνω, I overtake, apprehend

κατεσθίω, I eat up, devour

κλάω, I break (iconoclast, literally, a breaker of images)

κληρονόμος, -ου, ὁ, an heir

κτίζω, I create

λῃστής, -οῦ, ὁ, a robber

λύπη, -ης, ἡ, pain, grief

μοιχεύω, I commit adultery

νομίζω, I suppose

ξηραίνω, I dry up (cf. xerophagy, among early Christians, the practice of living on a diet of dry food, especially during Lent and other fasts)

ὅθεν, whence, wherefore

οἰκουμένη, -ης, ἡ, the (inhabited) world (cf. ecumenical)

ὁμοιόω, I make like, liken (homoeoteleuton, the occurrence of
the same or similar endings of lines, a frequent
source of error in copied manuscripts)

οὐδέποτε, never

παρθένος, -ου, ἡ, a virgin (parthenogenesis)

παύομαι, I cease

ποτίζω, I give drink to

σαλεύω, I shake

σκάνδαλον, -ου, τό, a cause of stumbling (scandal)

συμφέρω, I bring together; impersonally, it is profitable

σφραγίζω, I seal (cf. sphragistics, the science of seals, their
history, age, distinctions, etc.)

τράπεζα, -ης, ἡ, a table (trapeze, so called from the square
or rectangle formed by the ropes and crossbar)

τύπος, -ου, ὁ, mark, example (type)

ὑπακοή, -ῆς, ἡ, obedience

χόρτος, -ου, ὁ, grass, hay

ὠφελέω, I profit

WORDS OCCURRING 14 TIMES

ἄκανθαι, -ῶν, αἱ, thorns (the acanthus plant)

ἀλλότριος, -α, -ον, another's, strange

ἀμφότεροι, -αι, -α, both

ἀνάκειμαι, I recline (at meals)

ἀναχωρέω, I depart

ἀνθίστημι, I resist

ἀνομία, -ας, ἡ, lawlessness

ἅπαξ, once, once for all

ἀπειθέω, I disbelieve, disobey

ἀτενίζω, I look intently, gaze upon intently

ἀφίστημι, I withdraw, depart

γράμμα, -ατος, τό, a letter (of the alphabet); plural, writings

διαλογισμός, -οῦ, ὁ, a reasoning, questioning (cf. dialogue)

ἕκτος, -η, -ον, sixth

ἐλάχιστος, -η, -ον, least

ἐνιαυτός, -οῦ, ὁ, a year

ἐπίσταμαι, I understand (cf. epistemology, the science of the
         methods and grounds of knowledge)

εὐφραίνω, I rejoice (cf. Euphrosyne, one of the three Graces
         in Greek mythology)

θρίξ, τριχός, ἡ, a hair (trichina, a thread-like worm)

κατανοέω, I observe

κληρονομία, -ας, ἡ, an inheritance

κοινός, -ή, -όν, common, unclean (ceremonially)

κοινόω, I make common, I defile (ceremonially) (cf. cenobite,
         one dwelling in a convent community [where all is
         held in common])

κωφός, -ή, -όν, deaf, dumb

λύχνος, -ου, ὁ, a lamp

μακρόθεν, from afar, afar

μακροθυμία, -ας, ἡ, long-suffering, patience, forbearance

μερίζω, I divide

μέτρον, -ου, τό, a measure (meter)

μύρον, -ου, τό, ointment

μωρός, -ά, -όν, foolish (moron)

νοέω, I understand (noetic)

ξένος, -η, -ον, strange; as a noun, a stranger, host (the
         chemical element xenon)

οἷος, -α, -ον, such as

ὄφις, -εως, ὁ, a serpent (Ophites, Gnostics who revered the

serpent as the symbol of hidden, divine wisdom)

ὀψία, -ας, ἡ, evening

πετεινά, -ῶν, τά, birds

προσδέχομαι, I receive, wait for

σεισμός, -οῦ, ὁ, an earthquake (seismograph)

σῖτος, -ου, ὁ, wheat (parasite, literally, one who sits by
　　　　　[παρά] another's food and eats at his expense)

στηρίζω, I establish

τάλαντον, -ου, τό, a talent (talent)

ταπεινόω, I humble

φρόνιμος, -η, -ον, prudent

χωλός, -ή, -όν, lame

WORDS OCCURRING 13 TIMES

ἀθετέω, I reject (athetize, to reject a text or passage as
　　　　　spurious)

ἀνά, with the acc., upwards, up; with numerals, each; ἀνὰ μέσον,
　　　　　into the midst, among

ἀναγγέλλω, I announce, report

ἀναλαμβάνω, I take up

ἀναστροφή, -ῆς, ἡ, conduct

ἄνωθεν, from above, again

ἁρπάζω, I seize

αὔριον, tomorrow

βοάω, I cry aloud

βουλή, -ῆς, ἡ, counsel, purpose

δαιμονίζομαι, I am demon possessed (demonize)

διαλέγομαι, I dispute (dialectics)

διαφέρω, I differ

δράκων, -οντος, ὁ, a dragon (dragon)

εἶτα, then

ἐκπλήσσομαι, I am astonished, amazed

ἐλεημοσύνη, -ης, ἡ, alms (eleemosynary; alms)

ἐμπαίζω, I mock

ἕξ, six (Hexapla, the edition of the Old Testament compiled
by Origen, in the 3rd century, comprising six columns)

ἐξαποστέλλω, I send forth

ἔξωθεν, with the gen., from without

ἐπιζητέω, I seek for

ἐπιπίπτω, I fall upon

ζύμη, -ης, ἡ, leaven (enzyme)

θερισμός, -οῦ, ὁ, harvest (cf. thermal)

θύω, I sacrifice, kill

καπνός, -οῦ, ὁ, smoke

καταισχύνω, I put to shame

κατακαίω, I burn up

καταντάω, I come to

καταρτίζω, I mend, fit, perfect

κλέπτω, I steal (cf. cleptomania)

παιδεύω, I teach, chastise (cf. pedagogue)

παιδίσκη, -ης, ἡ, a maid servant

παράδοσις, -εως, ἡ, a tradition

πρίν, before

πώς, at all, somehow, in any way

συνεργός, -οῦ, ὁ, a fellow worker (cf. synergism, the Semi-
Pelagian doctrine that there are two efficient agents
in regeneration, namely the human will and the divine
Spirit, which, in the strict sense of the term, co-
operate)

τίμιος, -α, -ον, precious, honorable (cf. Timothy, honoring
God)

τρόπος, -ου, ὁ, manner, way (in rhetoric, trope, a figurative use of a word)

τύπτω, I smite (cf. tympanum, the middle ear)

ὕψιστος, -η, -ον, highest

φύσις, -εως, ἡ, nature (physics)

χρυσίον, -ου, τό, gold (cf. chrysanthemum, literally, golden
flower)

Words Occurring 12 Times

ἄδικος, -ον, unjust

ἀλέκτωρ, -ορος, ὁ, a cock (cf. alectryomancy, divination by
means of a cock encircled by grains of corn placed
on letters of the alphabet, the letters being then
put together in the order in which the grains were
eaten)

ἀναπαύω, I refresh; middle, I take rest

ἀναπίπτω, I recline

ἀπαρνέομαι, I deny

ἀσκός, -οῦ, ὁ, a (leather) bottle, wine-skin (in botany, as-
cidium, the leaf of the pitcher plant)

αὐλή, -ῆς, ἡ, a court (in Austro-German history, the Aulic
Council)

βαπτιστής, -οῦ, ὁ, baptist (Baptist)

βασανίζω, I torment

βῆμα, -ατος, τό, judgment seat (in ecclesiastical architec-
ture, bema, the inner part of the chancel, reserved
for the clergy)

βροντή, -ῆς, ἡ, thunder (brontosaurus, literally, thunder-
lizard)

γέεννα, -ης, ἡ, gehenna (Gehenna)

γόνυ, -ατος, τό, a knee (akin to genuflect)

δεῦτε, come!

44

διάνοια, -ας, ἡ, the mind, understanding, a thought

δίκτυον, -ου, τό, a net

ἔθος, -ους, τό, a custom (ethics)

ἐξάγω, I lead out

ἐξουθενέω, I despise

ἔσωθεν, from within, within

καίω, I burn (caustic)

κάλαμος, -ου, ὁ, a reed (calamus)

κολλάομαι, I join, cleave to (cf. colloid)

κομίζω, I receive

κράτος, -ους, τό, power, dominion (cf. democracy, rule of the
people)

λίαν, greatly

λιμός, -οῦ, ὁ, hunger, famine (in medicine, limosis, excessive
and morbid hunger)

λυχνία, -ας, ἡ, a lampstand

μάλιστα, especially

νήπιος, -ου, ὁ, an infant, child

οἰκοδεσπότης, -ου, ὁ, a householder

ὅραμα, -ατος, τό, a vision (panorama, a complete [πᾶν] view)

ὅρια, -ων, τά, boundries (cf. horizon)

παραιτέομαι, I make excuse, refuse

πιάζω, I take

πλουτέω, I am rich (cf. plutocrat)

πόρνη, -ης, ἡ, a prostitute (pornography)

πρόθεσις, -εως, ἡ, a setting forth; a purpose (in the Eastern
Church, the prothesis, referring to the placing of the
eucharistic elements)

προσλαμβάνω, I receive

πρωΐ, in the morning, early

πῶλος, -ου, ὁ, a colt

ῥάβδος, -ου, ἡ, a staff, rod (rhabdomancy, divination by rods)

σαλπίζω, I sound a trumpet

σπλαγχνίζομαι, I have compassion

σπουδή, -ῆς, ἡ, haste, diligence

στήκω, I stand, stand fast

συνέχω, I hold fast, oppress

ταχύ, quickly (tachygraphy, stenography, especially that of
        the ancient Greeks and Romans)

τυγχάνω, I obtain, happen

ὑγιαίνω, I am in good health (cf. hygiene)

ὑγιής, -ές, whole, healthy (cf. hygiene)

ὑψηλός, -ή, -όν, high

φιάλη, -ης, ἡ, a cup, bowl (phial, vial)

φονεύω, I kill, murder

χοῖρος, -ου, ὁ, a pig

χωρίζω, I separate, depart

ψεύδομαι, I lie (pseudo-)

WORDS OCCURRING 11 TIMES

ἀγαλλιάω, I exult

ἀγορά, -ᾶς, ἡ, a market-place (agora)

ἅλυσις, -εως, ἡ, a chain

ἀναστρέφω, I return; I live

ἀπιστία, -ας, ἡ, unbelief

ἀρχαῖος, -α, -ον, old, ancient (archaic)

ἄφρων, -ον, foolish

βρῶσις, -εως, ἡ, eating, food, rust

γέμω, I fill

δάκρυ, -υος, and δάκρυον, -ου, τό, a tear (akin to lachrymal)

διαμερίζω, I divide, distribute

δόλος, -ου, ὁ, guile

δωρεά, -ᾶς, ἡ, a gift

ἐάω, I permit

εἴδωλον, -ου, τό, an image, idol (idol)

εἴκοσι, twenty (icosahedron, a geometric figure with twenty
      faces)

εἰσάγω, I lead in

ἐκχύννομαι, I pour out

ἔλαιον, -ου, τό, olive-oil (akin to oil, oleo-)

ἐλευθερία, -ας, ἡ, liberty

ἐμβλέπω, I look at

ἐνδείκνυμαι, I show forth

ἔπαινος, -ου, ὁ, praise

ἐπαισχύνομαι, I am ashamed

ἐπισκέπτομαι, I visit, have a care for (cf. episcopal)

ζηλόω, I am zealous, pursue (cf. zeal)

ζωοποιέω, I make alive

θανατόω, I put to death (cf. thanatopsis)

θάπτω, I bury (cf. cenotaph; epitaph)

κακία, -ας, ἡ, malice, evil

καταβολή, -ῆς, ἡ, a foundation (cf. katabolism)

κατάκειμαι, I lie down, lie sick, recline (at meals)

κατασκευάζω, I prepare

κάτω, down, below

καύχημα, -ατος, τό, a boasting, ground of boasting

καύχησις, -εως, ἡ, boasting

κέρας, -ατος, τό, horn (rhinoceros, literally, nose-horn)

κλάδος, -ου, ὁ, a branch (of a tree) (in botany, cladophyll)

κλῆρος, -ου, ὁ, a lot (that which is cast or drawn); a portion
        (clergy; cleric, clerk)

κλῆσις, -εως, ἡ, a (divine) call, invitation, summons

κλητός, -ή, -όν, called

κράβαττος, -ου, ὁ, a bed, mattress, mat (of a poor man)

λίμνη, -ης, ἡ, a lake (limnology, the scientific study of
      ponds and lakes)

μεταβαίνω, I depart

νεανίσκος, -ου, ὁ, a youth

νόσος, -ου, ἡ, a disease (nosophobia, a morbid fear of
      disease)

ὀδούς, -όντος, ὁ, a tooth (odontology)

ὁμοθυμαδόν, with one accord

ὀνειδίζω, I reproach

παράγω, I pass by

παραλυτικός, -οῦ, ὁ, a paralytic (paralytic)

παρεμβολή, -ῆς, ἡ, a camp, army, fortress

περισσοτέρως, more abundantly

πηγή, -ῆς, ἡ, a spring, fountain

πληθύνω, I multiply

ποιμαίνω, I shepherd, rule (poimenic, pertaining to pastoral
      theology)

πρᾶγμα, -ατος, τό, a deed, matter, thing (pragmatic)

πρότερος, -α, -ον, former; as an adverb, before (cf. proto-)

πυνθάνομαι, I inquire

σάλπιγξ, -ιγγος, ἡ, a trumpet

σπλάγχνα, -ων, τά, bowels; heart, tender mercies, compassion

σπουδάζω, I endeavor, am diligent

σφόδρα, exceedingly

σχίζω, I split (schism; schizophrenia)

τελευτάω, I die

τριάκοντα, indeclinable, thirty

τρίς, thrice (in liturgics, the Trisagion)

ὑμέτερος, -α, -ον, your

ὑπαντάω, I meet, go to meet

ὕστερον, *later, afterwards* (in rhetoric, *hysteron*-proteron, a reversing of the natural order of the sense, as 'he is well and lives')

φυτεύω, *I plant*

φωτίζω, *I give light, enlighten* (cf. *photo-*)

χίλιοι, -αι, -α, *a thousand* (chiliasm, millenarianism)

χιτών, -ῶνος, ὁ, *a tunic* (chiton)

χράομαι, *I use* (catachresis, misuse of a word; in rhetoric, a mixed metaphor)

χρυσός, -οῦ, ὁ, *gold* (chrysanthemum)

ψευδοπροφήτης, -ου, ὁ, *a false prophet*

WORDS OCCURRING 10 TIMES

ἁγιασμός, -οῦ, ὁ, *sanctification*

ᾅδης, -ου, ὁ, **Hades** (Hades)

ἀδύνατος, -ον, *incapable, impossible*

ἀκαθαρσία, -ας ἡ, *uncleanness*

ἅμα, *at the same time;* with the dat., *together with*

ἀνατολή, -ῆς, ἡ, *east, dawn* (Anatolia)

ἀναφέρω, *I bring up, offer*

ἄνομος, -ον, *lawless, without law*

ἀπολογέομαι, *I defend myself* (cf. *apology*)

ἀπολύτρωσις, -εως, ἡ, *redemption*

ἀσπασμός, -οῦ, ὁ, *a greeting*

ἀφαιρέω, *I take away* (aphaeresis, dropping of a letter or syllable from the beginning of a word, as 'lone' from 'alone')

ἀφορίζω, *I separate* (aphorism)

βίβλος, -ου, ἡ, *a book* (Bible)

βίος, -ου, ὁ, *life* (biology)

δεσπότης, -ου, ὁ, *a master, lord* (despot)

διατρίβω, *I continue* (*diatribe*, a prolonged and acrimonious harangue)

δικαίωμα, -ατος, τό, *judgment*

διωγμός, -οῦ, ὁ, *persecution*

ἐκκόπτω, *I cut out, cut off*

ἐκπίπτω, *I fall away*

ἐμφανίζω, *I manifest*

ἔνατος, -η, -ον, *ninth* (*Ennead*, one division of the collection made by Porphyry of the teachings of Plotinus, arranged in six divisions of nine books each)

ἔνοχος, -ον, *involved in, liable, guilty*

ἐξομολογέομαι, *I confess, profess* (in the ancient Church, *exomologesis*, the public confession of sin, usually accompanied by fasting, weeping, and mourning)

ἐπειδή, *since, because*

ἐπιδίδωμι, *I give to*

ἐπιτάσσω, *I command*

ἐπιτελέω, *I complete, perform*

θλίβω, *I press, oppress*

ἰσχύς, -ύος, ἡ, *strength*

κοινωνός, -οῦ, ὁ, *a partner, sharer* (cf. cenobite, one dwelling in a convent community)

κοσμέω, *I adorn* (*cosmetics*)

μακράν, *far away*

μακροθυμέω, *I am patient*

μέλει, *it is a care*

νομικός, -ή, -όν, *pertaining to the law; as a noun, one skilled in the Mosaic law, a lawyer*

ξενίζω, *I entertain* (a stranger); *I startle, bewilder*

ὅδε, ἥδε, τόδε, *this* (here)

οἰκονόμος, -ου, ὁ, a steward (economy)

ὀνομάζω, I name (cf. onomasticon, a collection of proper
        names)

ὄντως, really (cf. ontology)

ὅρκος, -ου, ὁ, an oath

παντοκράτωρ, -ορος, ὁ, a ruler of all, the Almighty

πατάσσω, I smite

πενθέω, I mourn

περιστερά, -ᾶς, ἡ, a dove

πλάνη, -ης, ἡ, a wandering, error (cf. planet, which to the
        ancients was apparently a wandering celestial body)

πλατεῖα, -ας, ἡ, a street (place)

πλεονεξία, -ας, ἡ, covetousness

ποικίλος, -η, -ον, varied, manifold

πόρνος, -ου, ὁ, a fornicator (pornography)

προέρχομαι, I go in front, precede

προσκαρτερέω, I continue in or with

πύλη, -ης, ἡ, a gate, porch (pylon)

σέβομαι, I reverence, worship

σιωπάω, I am silent (aposiopesis, in rhetoric, a figure of
        speech in which the speaker breaks off suddenly)

στρατηγός, -οῦ, ὁ, a commander

συγγενής, -ές, kindred; as a noun, a relative, kinsman

σύνδουλος, -ου, ὁ, a fellow slave

συνζητέω, I question with, discuss

σφάζω, I slay

τάσσω, I arrange, appoint, order

ταχέως, quickly (cf. tachygraphy)

τέταρτος, -η, -ον, fourth (cf. tetrarch, a ruler over a
        fourth part)

ὑπόδημα, -ατος, τό, a sandal, shoe

φείδομαι, I spare

χρηστότης, -ητος, ἡ, goodness, kindness

χωρίον, -ου, τό, a place, field (cf. chorography, describing,
   or description, of districts)

ψεῦδος, -ους, τό, a lie (cf. pseudo-)

ψεύστης, -ου, ὁ, a liar (cf. pseudo-)

Total number of Greek words (other than proper
names) which occur in the New Testament ten
times or more. 1055

PART II

Words Classified according to their Root

After the student has mastered about four or five hundred words of frequent occurrence in the Greek Testament, he can be-begin to use with profit the following groups of words arranged according to their root. Here are collected those words, scattered throughout Part I, which are related to each other by reason of a common etymology. Each group was formed in accord with the requirement that it must contain at least three words each of which occurs ten times or more in the New Testament. In addition to such words from Part I which satisfy this arbitrary requirement, there have been added about 250 other words, each of which occurs from five to nine times in the New Testament. It will be discovered that these words of comparatively infrequent occurrence can be learned with very little additional effort when they are thus grouped with others derived from the same root.

The Formation of Words

Words do not grow haphazardly or in isolation from the rest of the vocabulary. To see how verbs, nouns, adjectives, adverbs, and particles can be traced to a relatively few basic roots is not only a fascinating study in itself, but it also lessens quite considerably the drudgery of piecemeal memorization of individual words. Thus, for example, the root ΤΕΛ, meaning *end*, forms the noun τέλος with the same meaning. From the noun a verb is produced, τελέω, meaning *I finish* or *fulfill* (that is, *I make an appropriate end*). From the noun comes also the adjective τέλειος, meaning *complete, perfect, mature* (that is, *brought to its appropriate end*). The adjective, again, is made into the verb τελειόω, which means *I complete, make perfect* — being equivalent to τέλειον ποιέω. Moreover, the same root ΤΕΛ appears in τελευτάω, a verb formed ultimately from τέλος and which means *I die* (that is, *I come to the end [of my life]*). Finally, to complete the list of all the words from this root which appear in the New Testament five times or more, by composition with prepositions the compound words ἐπιτελέω, συντέλεια, and συντελέω are formed, each of which involves some aspect of the root idea of *end*.

This example illustrates the principle of the building of Greek words. The root is the primitive part of the word. It conveys the meaning or abstract idea apart from its relations. From the root there are produced various verb-stems and noun-stems (the latter of which produce both nouns and adjectives). These stems are built (1) by the addition of various suffixes and (2) by an internal modification of the stem. The following is a simplified classification of some of the more important ways in which the words of the Greek Testament are formed. For a more complete technical description, any large reference grammar of New Testament Greek should be consulted.[1]

The suffix is a formative element standing between the root and the declensional or conjugational ending. Suffixes limit or particularize the general meaning of the root. Some suffixes [2]

---

[1] The best treatment is that by J.H.Moulton and W.F.Howard, *A Grammar of New Testament Greek*, vol. II, *Accidence and Word-Formation* (Edinburgh, 1929), pp. 268-410.

[2] It should be noted that roots, stems, and suffixes never existed as independent words in Greek, or indeed in any known period of the parent language from which Greek and the other Indo-European tongues were derived. The analysis of words into their component morphological elements is merely a scientific device useful for purposes of arrangement and classification.

have special meanings, and when these are known it is relatively easy to deduce the significance of an unfamiliar Greek word by analyzing the root idea in the stem as modified by the suffix.

A. Suffixes Forming Nouns

These suffixes are listed with the ending of the nominative case, singular number, attached. The figure within the parentheses following the suffix indicates the declension of the nouns formed with that suffix.

1. The *agent* is indicated by -της (1).

Examples: βαπτισ-τής (from βαπτίζω), *one who baptizes, a baptizer, baptist*

μαθη-τής (from μανθάνω), *one who learns, a learner, disciple*

2. An *action* is indicated by -μος (2) and -σις (3). The latter suffix often produces the abstract name of an action.

Examples: βαπτισ-μός (from βαπτίζω), *a washing, purification* (the act of which βάπτισμα is the result; see below)

καθαρισ-μός (from καθαρίζω), *a cleansing, purification*

ἀπολύτρω-σις (from ἀπολυτρόω, *I release on payment of a ransom*), *a releasing effected by payment of a ransom* (λύτρον), *redemption*

δικαίω-σις (from δικαιόω), *an act of adjudging one to be righteous, justification*

3. The *result* of an action is indicated by -μα (3).

Examples: βάπτισ-μα (from βαπτίζω), *baptism* (the abiding fact resulting from the act of baptism)

γράμ-μα (from γράφω), *thing written, a letter* (of the alphabet)

κήρυγ-μα (from κηρύσσω), *thing proclaimed by*

a herald, preaching

4. The abstract idea of *quality* is indicated by -ια (1),
-οτης (3), and -συνη (1).

> Examples: σοφ-ία, *wisdom*
>
> σωτηρ-ία, *salvation*
>
> κυρι-ότης, *lordship, dominion*
>
> νε-ότης, *youth*
>
> ἀγαθω-σύνη, *goodness*
>
> δικαιο-σύνη, *righteousness*

B. Suffixes Forming Adjectives

1. Adjectives expressing the meaning *of* or *belonging to*
a person or thing are formed by adding the suffix -ιος to a
noun-stem.

> Examples: οὐράν-ιος, *heavenly* (from οὐρανός, *heaven*)
>
> πλούσ-ιος, *wealthy* (from πλοῦτος, wealth)
>
> τίμ-ιος, *precious, honorable* (from τιμή,

honor, price)

2. Adjectives expressing the idea *belonging to, pertaining to, with the characteristics of*, are formed by adding the
suffix -ικος to a noun-stem.

> Examples: βασιλ-ικός, *belonging to a king, kingly,*
royal (from βασιλεύς, *a king*)
>
> πνευματ-ικός, *pertaining to the spirit, with*
the characteristics of the spirit, spiritual (from πνεῦμα,
spirit)
>
> σαρκ-ικός, *fleshly, carnal* (from σάρξ, *flesh*)
>
> σωματ-ικός, *pertaining to the body, bodily*
(from σῶμα, *body*)

3. Adjectives which express the *material* from which anything is made are formed with the suffix -ινος.

Examples: δερμάτ-ινος, *of skin, leathern*
　　　　　λίθ-ινος, *of stone*
　　　　　σάρκ-ινος, *of the flesh*

4. Many other adjectival suffixes have no characteristic signification. Some of these are -ος, -λος, -νος, -ανος, -μος, and -ρος.

5. A special class of adjectives, called verbal adjectives, is formed by the suffix -τος. These either (a) have the meaning of a perfect passive participle or (b) express *possibility*.

Examples: (a) ἀγαπη-τός, *beloved*
　　　　　　　εὐλογη-τός, *blessed*
　　　　　　　κρυπ-τός, *hidden*
　　　　　(b) ἀνεκ-τός, *bearable, tolerable*

In general the passive sense is more common. Some have either signification, as ἀδύνα-τος, *incapable* or *impossible*.

C. Suffixes Forming Verbs

From the original verb-stem, which is ordinarily preserved unchanged in the second aorist stem, the present stem is formed in various ways, some of which are the following. It will be observed that not only are suffixes employed but that also an internal modification of the stem may take place (called *Ablaut*).

1. The verb-stem may remain unchanged.
Examples: ἄγ-ω, *I lead*
　　　　　δέ-ω, *I bind*
　　　　　λύ-ω, *I loose*

2. The initial consonant of the verb-stem may undergo reduplication.
Examples: γίνομαι, *I become*, from the stem γεν-

(classical γίγνομαι, from *γι-γέν-ομαι)[3]

δί-δω-μι, *I give*, from the stem δο-

ἵ-στη-μι *I cause to stand*, from the stem στα-
(for *σί-στη-μι)

πίπτω, *I fall*, from the stem πετ- (for *πι-πέτ-ω)

3. The vowel in the verb-stem may be lengthened.

Examples: λείπ-ω, *I leave*, from λιπ- (cf. 2nd aor. ἔ-λιπ-ον)

πείθ-ω, *I persuade*, from πιθ- (cf. 2nd aor. ἔ-πιθ-ον)

φεύγ-ω, *I flee*, from φυγ- (cf. 2nd aor. ἔ-φυγ-ον)

4. The final consonant of the verb-stem may be doubled.

Examples: ἀπο-στέλλ-ω, *I send away*, from στελ-

βάλλ-ω, *I throw*, from βαλ- (cf. 2nd aor. ἔ-βαλ-ον)

5. Another consonant may be added to the verb-stem, as -ν-, -σκ-, or -τ-.

Examples: θνή-σκω, *I die*, from θαν- (cf. 2nd aor. ἔ-θαν-ον)

πί-νω, *I drink*, from πι- (cf. 2nd aor. ἔ-πι-ον)

τύπ-τω, *I strike*, from τυπ- (cf. 2nd aor. ἔ-τυπ-ον)

6. An additional syllable may be added to the verb-stem.

a. The ending -άνω, sometimes with ν (μ before a labial) inserted in the verb-stem, may be added.

Examples: ἁμαρτ-άνω, *I sin*, from ἁμαρτ- (cf. 2nd aor.

---

[3] An asterisk preceding a Greek word here and in the list below signifies that this form, though preserved in no extant source, must be postulated as the parent of existing forms.

ἥμαρτ-ον)

μανθ-άνω, I learn, from μαθ- (cf. 2nd aor.
ἔ-μαθ-ον)

b. The endings -άζω, -ίζω, or -ύζω may be added.

Examples: λιθ-άζω, I stone

ἐλπ-ίζω, I hope

γογγ-ύζω, I grumble, murmur

c. The endings -άω, -έω, or -εύω may be added. These usually denote an action or state similar to that expressed by the noun-stem.

Examples· ἀγαπ-άω, I love, from ἀγάπη, love

δουλ-εύω, I serve (as a slave), from δοῦλος, a slave

φιλ-έω, I love, am friendly towards, from φίλος, a friend

d. The endings -αίνω, -όω, or -ύνω may be added. These usually express causation, except in verbs of mental action such as ἀξι-όω, I deem worthy, δικαι-όω, I deem or judge or pronounce righteous.

Examples: δουλ-όω, I enslave, from δοῦλος, a slave

πικρ-αίνω, I make bitter, embitter, from πικρός, sharp, bitter

πληθ-ύνω, (transitive) I multiply, (intransitive) I abound, from πλῆθος, a throng

e. Some Greek verbs are 'irregular,' that is, their present stem is entirely different from their aorist stem (and frequently other stems likewise). Thus, φέρω means I carry, but ἤνεγκα means I carried; ἐσθίω means I eat, ἔφαγον means I ate. The reason for the existence of these irregular verbs is simply that the aorist tense of one verb and the present tense of another verb of quite similar meaning both fell into disuse. The remaining present and aorist tenses of these two verbs then came to be associated together as though they were related etymologically. The same thing has happened in languages other than Greek. In English the verb *went* is not the etymological preterit of *go;* it is the past tense of the little used verb *wend*. Further, modern English rejects the former preterit of *go* (the Anglo-Saxon *éode* and Middle English *yode*). The tenses that remain of each verb now function as the principal parts of one verb. In French, to take an example of irregularity within the same tense, the first and second persons plural of the present tense of the verb *aller*, to go, are *nous allons, vous allez,* but the other forms of the present tense are *je vais, tu vas,* etc. The conjugation of the verb is irregular because behind the different forms lie two different Latin words which, for some reason, came to be preferred in those persons (they are *ambulare* and *vadare,* both meaning 'to walk, go').[4]

The irregular verbs which (with their compounds) occur most frequently in the Greek New Testament are the following. A hyphen before a principal part means that this form appears only in compound verbs.

αἱρέω, *I take,* middle, *I choose,* fut. αἱρήσομαι and -ελῶ, 2nd aor. -εῖλον, middle εἱλάμην, perf. -ῄρημαι, aor. passive -ῃρέθην.

εἶπον and εἶπα, *I said,* fut. ἐρῶ, perf. εἴρηκα, perf. passive εἴρημαι, aor. passive ἐρρέθην and ἐρρήθην.

ἔρχομαι, *I come, go,* fut. ἐλεύσομαι, 2nd aor. ἦλθον, perf. ἐλήλυθα.

ἐσθίω and ἔσθω, *I eat,* fut. φάγομαι, 2nd aor. ἔφαγον.

---

[4] The Italian verb *andare* exhibits the same irregularity: *noi andiamo, voi andate,* but *io vado, tu vai,* etc.

ὁράω, *I see*, fut. ὄψομαι, 2nd aor. εἶδον, perf. ἑώρακα
and ἑόρακα, aor. passive ὤφθην.

τρέχω, *I run*, 2nd aor. ἔδραμον.

φέρω, *I carry*, fut. οἴσω, aor. ἤνεγκα and -ἤνεγκον,
perf. -ενήνοχα, aor. passive ἠνέχθην.

COMPOUND WORDS

Everything set forth above refers to the building of simple words from one stem. Compound words, on the other hand, are
formed from a union of two or more stems or parts, as ψευδοπροφήτης, *a false prophet*, and ἀντι-παρ-ῆλθεν, *he passed by*
[παρά] *on the other side* [ἀντί], used of the priest and the
Levite in the parable of the Good Samaritan (Luke 10:31f). As
can be observed from these two examples, a compound word contains a defining part and a defined part, usually in this order.
The parts of a compound word stand in various syntactical relations to each other, as that of adjective or attributive genitive to a noun, or that of adverb or object to a verb, etc.
Compounds may thus be regarded as abbreviated forms of syntax.
In analyzing the meaning of a compound, it must be kept in mind
that no part of the word is without significance.

Compound words are formed chiefly in the following three
ways.

1. Various particles and adverbs may be prefixed. The two
of most frequent occurrence are:

a. The alpha privative, ἀ- (before vowels generally ἀν-),
which gives a negative sense to the word to which it is affixed
(cf. the English prefix 'un-').

Examples: ἄ-δικος, *unjust*
ἀ-τιμάζω, *I dishonor*
ἀν-έγκλητος, *unreprovable, blameless*

b. The adverbial prefix εὐ-, which supplies the general idea of 'prosperously,' 'being well disposed.'

Examples: εὐ-δοκέω, *I am well pleased, think it good*

εὐ-λογέω, *I speak well of, praise, bless*

2. One or more prepositions may be prefixed. For detailed information regarding this very large class of compound verbs, see Appendix II, pp. 102ff.

3. Two or more noun-stems or verb-stems may be compounded. As regards their meaning, compound nouns (substantives and adjectives) may be divided into two principal classes.

a. Objective compounds. In these the first part is related to the other as a sort of grammatical object. When the two are expressed in English as separate words, the first is put in an oblique case depending, either immediately or by means of a preposition, on the other.

Examples: θεό-πνευστος, *inspired by God*

νομο-διδάσκαλος, *a teacher of [the] Law*

οἰκο-δεσπότης, *a master of a house, a householder*

b. Possessive and descriptive compounds. In these the first part qualifies the second like an adjective or adverb.

Examples: μακρο-θυμία, *long-suffering*

μον-όφθαλμος, *one-eyed, having one eye*

ὀλιγό-πιστος, *having little faith*

ταπεινο-φροσύνη, *lowliness of mind, humility*

In drawing up the following ninety-seven groups of words the author has tried to avoid two extremes. He has tried to refrain from spinning out fanciful derivations for the sake of establishing connections between words which, according to scientific linguistics, are entirely unrelated. No statement about

root or derivation is made which involves a descent to the
level of popular or folk-etymology. If a root is obscure or
uncertain — or even merely probable — it has not been given.[5]
The other extreme which he has tried to avoid is the cumbering
of the lists with technical details of advanced linguistics. It
may very well be, for example, that originally there was but
one root ΛΕΓ which meant 'gather, pick' as well as 'say,' but
it is not inaccurate to differentiate between the two by forming
two separate lists of words involving each of these meanings;
and certainly such an arrangement is less liable to engender
confusion than the other.

Finally, it ought to be mentioned that several of the roots
contain the obsolete Greek letter *vau*, Ϝ, called 'digamma' (i.e.
double-gamma) from its shape.[6] The sound of this letter was
like that of English *w*. Thus, the root ϜΙΔ, *see*, lies behind
εἶδον (for ε-ϝιδ-ον) and the second perfect tense οἶδα, *I know*
(literally, *I have seen*); compare other Indo-European words,
such as Sanskrit *ved-a, knowledge;* Latin *vid-eo, I see;* German
wis-sen, know; Anglo-Saxon *wit-an* (English *to wit* and the
archaic *wot* [means *know;* see Acts 3:17, Rom. 11:2, etc., in
the King James Version]).

[5] The chief authorities upon which the etymologies are based
are Walther Prellwitz, *Etymologisches Wörterbuch der griechischen
Sprache* (2nd ed., Göttingen, 1905), and Emile Boisacq, *Dictionnaire
étymologique de la langue grecque* (3rd ed., Heidelberg and Paris, 1938).

[6] *Vau* had not entirely disappeared in pronunciation when the
Homeric poems were composed, and the meter of many verses in these is
explained only by admitting its presence.

root ΑΓ, drive, lead, weigh

ἄγω, I lead

ἀνάγω, I lead up; middle, I put to sea, set sail

ἀπάγω, I lead away

εἰσάγω, I lead in, bring in

ἐξάγω, I lead out

παράγω, I pass by

περιάγω, I lead about, go about

προάγω, I lead forth, go before

συνάγω, I gather together

συναγωγή, -ῆς, ἡ, a synagogue

ἀρχισυνάγωγος, -ου, ὁ, a ruler of a synagogue

ἐπισυνάγω, I collect, gather together at one place

ὑπάγω, I depart

ἀγρός, -οῦ, ὁ, (place where cattle are led or driven), a field

ἡγέομαι, I am chief; (I lead through the mind), I think, regard

ἡγεμών, -όνος, ὁ, a leader, governor

ἄξιος, -α, -ον, (of equal weight), worthy

ἀξιόω, I deem worthy, think fit

ἀξίως, worthily

ἀγών, -ῶνος, ὁ, an athletic contest, a contest

root ʽΑΓ, religious awe, reverence

ἅγιος, -α, -ον, holy

ἁγιάζω, I make holy, sanctify

ἁγιασμός, -οῦ, ὁ, sanctification

ἁγνός, -ή, -όν, (in a condition prepared for worship), pure
     (ethically, ritually, or ceremonially), chaste

66

ἁγνίζω, I make pure

ἀγαπάω, I love
ἀγάπη, -ης, ἡ, love
ἀγαπητός, -ή, -όν, beloved

ἄγγελος, -ου, ὁ, a messenger, an angel
ἀναγγέλλω, I announce, report
ἀπαγγέλλω, I announce, report
ἐπαγγελία, -ας, ἡ, a promise
ἐπαγγέλλομαι, I promise
εὐαγγελίζω, I bring good news, preach good tidings (the Gospel)
εὐαγγέλιον, -ου, τό, good news, the Gospel
καταγγέλλω, I proclaim
παραγγέλλω, I command, charge
παραγγελία, -ας, ἡ, a charge, command

αἰτέω, I ask
αἰτία, -ας, ἡ, a cause, accusation
παραιτέομαι, I make excuse, refuse

ἀκούω, I hear
εἰσακούω, I hearken to, assent to
ὑπακούω, I obey
ἀκοή, -ῆς, ἡ, hearing, a report
ὑπακοή, -ῆς, ἡ, obedience

root ΑΛΛ, other

ἄλλος, -η, -ο, other, another
ἀλλήλων, (reduplicated stem, αλλ-ηλο), of one another

ἀλλά, (neuter plural with changed accent: 'in another way'),
    but

ἀλλάσσω, (I make other than it is), I change, alter

καταλλάσσω, I change (from enmity to friendship), reconcile

root ΑΡ, join, fit

ἀρέσκω, (I fit or join together; suit), I please

ἀριθμός, -οῦ, ὁ, a number

ἄρτι, (fitting exactly), now, just now

ἀρετή, -ῆς, ἡ, (moral fitness), virtue, excellence

root ΑΡΧ, be first

ἄρχω, (first in point of station), I rule; middle, (first in
    point of time), I begin

ἄρχων, -οντος, ὁ, a ruler

ἀρχή, -ῆς, ἡ, a beginning

ἀρχαῖος, -α, -ον, old, ancient

ἀρχιερεύς, -έως, ὁ, a chief priest, high priest

ὑπάρχω, (I am under as a foundation, support), I am, I exist,
    I belong to (τὰ ὑπάρχοντα, one's belongings, possessions)

ἀπαρχή, -ῆς, ἡ, first fruits

root ΒΛ, go

ἀναβαίνω, I go up

ἐμβαίνω, (I step into [a boat]), I embark

ἐπιβαίνω, I go up to, mount, board (a boat)

καταβαίνω, I go down

μεταβαίνω, I depart

παράβασις, -εως, ἡ, (a going over [the line]), transgression,
    a transgression

παραβάτης, -ου, ὁ, a transgressor

προβαίνω, I go forward, go on

πρόβατον, -ου, τό, a sheep (that which goes forward)

συμβαίνω, (of events) happen, occur

βῆμα, -ατος, τό, judgment seat (that which the judge mounts)

βέβαιος, -α, -ον, (reduplicated stem, βε-βα-, standing fast),
    solid, sure, firm

βεβαιόω, I confirm, ratify

βέβηλος, -η, -ον, (lawful to be trodden), profane, secular

root ΒΑΛ, throw

βάλλω, I throw, put

ἐκβάλλω, I cast out

ἐπιβάλλω, I lay upon

λιθοβολέω, I pelt with stones, kill by stoning

περιβάλλω, I put around, clothe

συμβάλλω, (I throw together), I encounter, meet, consider;
    middle, contribute to

ὑπερβάλλω, (I surpass in throwing), I surpass, exceed

διάβολος, -ου, ὁ, (one who throws across or at, with words, a
    slanderer), the accuser, the Devil

καταβολή, -ῆς, -ἡ, (that which is put down), a foundation

παραβολή, -ῆς, ἡ (a placing of one thing by the side of another,
    by way of comparison), a parable

παρεμβολή, -ῆς, ἡ, a camp, army, fortress

ὑπερβολή, -ῆς, ἡ, (a throwing beyond), excess, abundance

———————————

βασιλεύς, -έως, ὁ, a king

βασιλεύω, I reign

βασιλεία, -ας, ἡ, a kingdom

βασιλικός, -ή, -όν, kingly, royal

root ΒΑΦ, dip

βαπτίζω, I baptize

βάπτισμα, -ατος, τό, baptism

βαπτιστής, -οῦ, ὁ, baptizer, Baptist (used only of John)

βλέπω, I see

ἀναβλέπω, I look up, receive sight

ἐμβλέπω, I look at

περιβλέπομαι, I look around, survey

root ΓΕΝ, beget, become

γίνομαι, (Attic, γίγνομαι, a reduplicated form, =*γι-γέν-ομαι),

   I become, come into being, happen, am made, am

παραγίνομαι, I come, arrive

γονεύς, -έως, ὁ, a parent

γένος, -ους, τό, race, kind

μονογενής, -ές, only-begotten, only

συγγενής, -ές, kindred, relative, kinsman

γενεά, -ᾶς, ἡ, a generation

γένεσις, -εως, ἡ, birth, origin

γένημα, -ατος, τό, fruit, produce

γεννάω, I beget

γυνή, γυναικός, ἡ, a woman, wife

γαμέω, I marry

γάμος, -ου, ὁ, a marriage, wedding

root ΓΝΩ, know

γινώσκω, *I know*

ἀναγινώσκω, *(I know again), I read*

ἐπιγινώσκω, *I come to know, recognize*

γνῶσις, -εως, ἡ, *wisdom*

ἐπίγνωσις, -εως, ἡ, *knowledge*

προγινώσκω, *I know beforehand, foreknow*

γνωρίζω, *I make known*

γνωστός, -ή, -όν, *known; as a noun, an acquaintance*

γνώμη, -ης, ἡ, *opinion, counsel*

ἀγνοέω, *I do not know*

root ΓΡΑΦ, scratch, scrape (signs in stone or wood)

γράφω, *I write*

γραφή, -ῆς, ἡ, *a writing, Scripture*

ἐπιγράφω, *I write upon, inscribe*

ἐπιγραφή, -ῆς, ἡ, *an inscription*

γράμμα, -ατος, τό, *a letter (of the alphabet), writing*

γραμματεύς, -έως, ὁ, *a scribe*

root ΔΕ, bind

δέω, *I bind*

δεῖ *(it is binding), it is necessary, one must*

δέσμιος, -ου, ὁ, *a prisoner*

δεσμός, -οῦ, ὁ, *a fetter, bond*

ὑπόδημα, -ατος, τό, *(that which is bound under [the foot]), a sandal, shoe*

root ΔΕΙΚ, show, point

δείκνυμι and δεικνύω, *I show*

ἐνδείκνυμαι, *I show forth*

ἐπιδείκνυμι, *I show, prove*

ὑποδείκνυμι, (*I show by placing under* [the eyes]), *I warn*
ὑπόδειγμα, -ατος, τό, *an example, copy*

root ΔΕΚ, take

δέχομαι, *I take, receive*
ἀποδέχομαι, *I accept from, receive, welcome*
ἐκδέχομαι, *I expect, wait for*
ἀπεκδέχομαι, *I wait for eagerly*
παραδέχομαι, *I accept, receive*
προσδέχομαι, *I receive, wait for*
εὐπρόσδεκτος, -ον, *well-received, acceptable*
προσδοκάω, *I wait for*
δεξιός, -ά, -όν, [δεκ +σ = δεξ], *right* (perhaps because the *right*
    hand is oftenest used in *taking*)

διάκονος, -ου, ὁ and ἡ, *a servant, deacon, deaconess*
διακονέω, *I serve, wait upon, care for one's needs, minister*
διακονία, -ας, ἡ, *the office and work of a* διάκονος, *service,*
    ministry

διδάσκω, *I teach*
διδάσκαλος, -ου, ὁ, *a teacher*
διδασκαλία, -ας, ἡ, *teaching*
διδαχή, -ῆς, ἡ, *teaching*

root ΔΙΚ, show, point

δίκαιος, -α, -ον, *righteous* (in accord with the way *pointed* out)
δικαιόω, *I justify, pronounce righteous*
δικαιοσύνη, -ης, ἡ, *righteousness*
δικαίωμα, -ατος, τό, *judgment*
δικαίως, *justly, uprightly*

ἐκδικέω, I avenge
ἀδικέω, I wrong, do wrong
ἄδικος, -ον, unjust
ἀδικία, -ας, ἡ, unrighteousness
ἀντίδικος, -ου, ὁ, an opponent in a suit at law, an adversary
ἐκδίκησις, -εως, ἡ, vengeance, punishment*

root ΔΟ, give

δίδωμι, I give
ἀποδίδωμι, I give back, pay; middle, I sell
ἀνταποδίδωμι, I give back (in return)
ἐπιδίδωμι, I give to
μεταδίδωμι, I share with, impart
παραδίδωμι, I hand over, betray
παράδοσις, -εως, ἡ, a tradition (that which has been handed over)
δωρεά, -ᾶς, ἡ, a gift
δωρεάν, (accusative of the noun, used adverbially: as a gift,
    gift-wise), freely
δῶρον, -ου, τό, a gift

root ΔΟΚ, beseem, befit

δοκέω, I think; I seem
εὐδοκέω, I think it good, am well pleased with
εὐδοκία, -ας, ἡ, good will, favor, pleasure, approval
συνευδοκέω, I entirely approve of, agree with
δόξα, -ης, ἡ, glory
δοξάζω, I glorify
δοκιμάζω, I prove, approve
ἀποδοκιμάζω, I reject (after testing)
δοκιμή, -ῆς, ἡ, a proving, approvedness, character
δόκιμος, -ον, tested, approved

ἀδόκιμος, -ον, (failing to pass the test), unapproved, counter-
   feit

δόγμα, -ατος, τό, a (public) decree

δοῦλος, -ου, ὁ, a slave

σύνδουλος, -ου, ὁ, a fellow slave

δουλεία, -ας, ἡ, slavery

δουλεύω, I serve

δουλόω, I enslave

δύναμαι, I am powerful, able

ἐνδυναμόω, I endue with power, make strong

δύνατος, -η, -ον, powerful, possible

ἀδύνατος, -ον, impossible

δύναμις, -εως, ἡ, power

ἔλεος, -ους, τό, pity, mercy

ἐλεέω, I have mercy

ἐλεημοσύνη, -ης, ἡ, alms

root ΕΡΧ, come, go

ἔρχομαι, I come, go

ἀπέρχομαι, I depart

διέρχομαι, I pass through

εἰσέρχομαι, I go in

ἐξέρχομαι, I go out

ἐπέρχομαι, I come upon (sometimes with hostility)

κατέρχομαι, I come down, go down

παρέρχομαι, I pass by, pass away

προέρχομαι, I go before

προσέρχομαι, I come to

συνέρχομαι, *I come together*

root ΕΣ, be

εἰμί, *I am*

ἄπειμι, *I am absent*

πάρειμι, *I am present; I have arrived*

παρουσία, -ας, ἡ, *presence, coming (especially Christ's [second]*
  coming in glory)

ἔξεστι, *it is permitted, it is lawful*

ἐξουσία, -ας, ἡ, *authority*

root ΕΧ and ΣΕΧ, have

ἔχω, *I have, hold*

ἀνέχομαι, *(I bear up), I endure*

ἀνεκτός, -όν, *bearable, tolerable*

ἀπέχω, *I have received (payment); I am distant*

ἐπέχω, *I hold out, give attention to*

κατέχω, *I hold fast, hold back*

μετέχω, *I have a share in, partake of*

μέτοχος, -ον, *sharing in; as a noun, a partner*

παρέχω, *I offer, afford*

προσέχω, *I attend to, give heed to*

συνέχω, *(I hold together, constrain), I hold fast, oppress*

ὑπερέχω, *(I hold over, above), I rise above, am superior*

ἔνοχος, -ον, *(=ἐνερχόμενος, held in, bound by), liable, guilty*

εὐσχήμων, -ον, *of elegant figure (way of holding oneself),*
  graceful, of good standing

μετασχηματίζω, *I change the figure of, transfigure*

root FEP, speak

ἐρῶ, *(from a rare present stem, εἴρω), I shall say*

ῥῆμα, -ατος, τό, *a word*

παρρησία, -ας, ή, boldness (of speech), confidence
παρρησιάζομαι, I speak boldly

root ϜΕΡΓ, work

ἔργον, -ου, τό, work
ἐργάτης, -ου, ὁ, a workman
ἐνεργέω, I work, effect
συνεργέω, I work along with, co-operate with
συνεργός, -οῦ, ὁ and ή, a fellow worker
ἐργάζομαι, I work
ἐργασία, -ας, ή, work, business, profit
κατεργάζομαι, I work out
γεωργός, -οῦ, ὁ, (a worker in the earth [γῆ]), a farmer
λειτουργός, -οῦ, ὁ, (a public [λαός] minister), a servant
πανουργία, -ας, ή, (ability to do anything, cleverness), crafti-
    ness, cunning
ἀργός, -όν, idle, lazy (contracted from ἀ-εργός)
καταργέω, I bring to naught, abolish

root ϜΙΔ, see

εἶδον, I saw
εἶδος, -ους, τό, visible form, shape
εἴδωλον, -ου, τό, an image, idol
εἰδωλολάτρης, -ου, ὁ, an idolater
οἶδα, (second perfect [I have seen] with present sense), I know
ᾅδης, -ου, ὁ, (α privative and Ϝιδ, the unseen world), Hades

ζάω, I live
ζωή, -ῆς, ή, life
ζῷον, -ου, τό, a living creature, an animal

ζητέω, I seek

ἐκζητέω, I seek out

ἐπιζητέω, I seek for

συνζητέω, I question with, discuss

ζήτημα, -ατος, τό, a question, debate

ζήτησις, -εως, ἡ, a questioning, debate

root ΘΑΝ, die

θνῄσκω, I die; perfect tense, I am dead

θνητός, -ή, -όν, liable to death, mortal

ἀποθνῄσκω, I die

θάνατος, -ου, ὁ, death

θανατόω, I put to death

root ΘΕ, put, set, place

τίθημι, I place,

ἀποτίθεμαι, I put off from myself, lay aside

διατίθημι, I appoint, make a covenant

ἐπιτίθημι, I lay upon

μετατίθημι, I transfer, change

παρατίθημι, I set before; middle, I entrust

περιτίθημι, I place around, clothe

προστίθημι, I add, I add to

ἀθετέω, I reject

θεμέλιος, -ον, as a noun, a foundation (the thing laid down)

θεμελιόω, I lay the foundation of, make stable

θησαυρός, οῦ, ὁ, a storehouse; treasure

θησαυρίζω, I store up, treasure up

ἀποθήκη, -ης, ἡ, a place in which anything is laid by, a storehouse, granary, barn

διαθήκη, -ης, ἡ, a covenant

ἀνάθεμα, -ατος, τό, (a thing laid by or set up; a thing
    devoted to the vengeance of God), *a curse, a man accursed*

root ΘΥ (1), burn, smoke

θύω, *I sacrifice, kill*

θυμίαμα, -ατος, τό, *incense*

θυσία, -ας, ἡ, *a sacrifice*

θυσιαστήριον, -ου, τό, (a place for sacrifice), *an altar*

root ΘΥ (2), rush

θυμός, -οῦ, ὁ, *wrath*

ἐπιθυμέω, (I have it upon my heart), *I desire*

ἐπιθυμία, -ας, ἡ, *eager desire, passion*

μακροθυμέω, *I am patient*

μακροθυμία, -ας, ἡ, *long-suffering*

ὁμοθυμαδόν, *with one accord*

προθυμία, -ας, ἡ, *eagerness, enthusiasm*

root 'Ι, set in motion

ἄνεσις, -εως, ἡ, *a loosening; relief, rest*

ἀφίημι, *I let go, permit, forgive*

ἄφεσις, -εως, ἡ, *a sending away, remission*

συνίημι, (I go along with), *I understand*

σύνεσις, -εως, ἡ, *understanding*

ἀσύνετος, -ον, *without understanding, stupid*

ἰσχύς, -ύος, ἡ, *strength*

ἰσχυρός, -ά, -όν, *strong*

ἰσχύω, *I am strong*

root ΚΑΘ, clean

καθαρός, -ά, -όν, clean

καθαρίζω, I cleanse

καθαρισμός, -οῦ, ὁ, a cleansing, purification

ἀκαθαρσία, -ας, ἡ, uncleanness

ἀκάθαρτος, -ον, unclean

root ΚΑΛ, call

καλέω, I call

κλητός, -ή, -όν, called

κλῆσις, -εως, ἡ, a (divine) call, invitation

ἐγκαλέω, I call to account, accuse

ἀνέγκλητος, -ον, not to be called to account, unreprovable,
   blameless

ἐκκλησία, -ας, ἡ, a Church, the Church

ἐπικαλέομαι, I call, name; middle, I invoke, appeal to

παρακαλέω, (I call beside myself), I beseech, exhort, console

παράκλησις, -εως, ἡ, exhortation, consolation

παράκλητος, -ου, ὁ, an intercessor, helper, Paraclete

προσκαλέομαι, I summon

συνκαλέω, I call together, assemble

καυχάομαι, I boast

καύχημα, -ατος, τό, a boasting, a ground of boasting

καύχησις, -εως, ἡ, boasting

root ΚΕΙ, lie outstretched

κεῖμαι, I lie

ἀνάκειμαι, I recline (at meals)

ἀντίκειμαι, I resist, oppose

ἐπίκειμαι, I lie upon, press upon, am urgent

κατάκειμαι, I lie down, lie sick; I recline (at meals)

περίκειμαι, I am compassed about with, have around me

πρόκειμαι, I am set before, am present

συνανάκειμαι, I recline together, feast together

κοιμάομαι, (I lie at rest), I sleep, fall asleep, die

κώμη, -ης, ἡ, a village

κλῆρος, -ου, ὁ, a lot, a portion

κληρονόμος, -ου, ὁ, an heir

κληρονομέω, I inherit

κληρονομία, -ης, ἡ, an inheritance

κοινός, -ή, -όν, common, unclean

κοινόω, I make common, defile

κοινωνέω, I have a share of, take part in

κοινωνία, -ας, ἡ, fellowship, collection

κοινωνός, -οῦ, ὁ and ἡ, a partner, sharer

root ΚΟΠ, cut, strike

κόπτω, I cut; middle, I strike (my breast or head in lamenta-
    tion

ἀποκόπτω, I cut off, amputate

ἐκκόπτω, I cut out, cut off

ἐνκόπτω, (I cut into), I block, hinder

προσκόπτω, I strike against, stumble, stumble at

πρόσκομμα, -ατος, τό, a stumbling, a stumbling block, an ob-
    stacle

κόπος, -ου, ὁ, trouble, labor

80

εὔκοπος, -ον, *with easy labor, easy*
κοπιάω, *I toil*

root ΚΡΑΤ and ΚΑΡΤ, strong, hard

κράτος, -ους, τό, *power, dominion*
κρατέω, *I grasp*
κρείσσων, (or κρείττων), -ονος, *better*
προσκαρτερέω, *I continue in or with*
παντοκράτωρ, -ορος, ὁ, *ruler of all, the Almighty*

root ΚΡΙ, separate

κρίνω, *I judge, decide*
ἀνακρίνω, *I examine*
ἀποκρίνομαι, *I answer*
διακρίνω, *I discriminate;* middle, *I doubt*
κατακρίνω, *I condemn*
κρίμα, -ατος, τό, *judgment*
κρίσις, -εως, ἡ, *judgment*
κριτής, -οῦ, ὁ, *a judge*
ὑποκριτής, -οῦ, ὁ, *a hypocrite (literally, a pretender, an actor)*
ὑπόκρισις, -εως, ἡ, *(acting a part), hypocrisy*
ἀνυπόκριτος, -ον, *unfeigned, undisguised*

root ΛΑΒ, take, receive

λαμβάνω, *I take, receive* (2nd aor., ἔ-λαβ-ον)
ἀναλαμβάνω, *I take up*
ἐπιλαμβάνω, *I take hold of*
καταλαμβάνω, *I undertake, apprehend*
μεταλαμβάνω, *I have a share of, partake of, get*
παραλαμβάνω, *I receive*

προσλαμβάνω, *I receive*

συλλαμβάνω, *I take, conceive*

ὑπολαμβάνω, *I take up (by supporting beneath); I welcome;*
   I catch up (in speech); *I suppose*

root ΛΑΘ, conceal

λανθάνω, *I am hidden from, escape notice* (2nd aor., ἔ-λαθ-ον)

ἐπιλανθάνομαι, *I forget, neglect*

ἀληθής, -ές, *true (not concealed)*

ἀληθινός, -ή, -όν, *true*

ἀλήθεια, -ας, ἡ, *truth*

ἀληθῶς, *truly,*

root ΛΕΓ (1), gather, pick

διαλέγομαι, *(I pick out [thoughts] one from another), I dispute*

διάλεκτος, -ου, ἡ, *speech, language*

ἐκλέγομαι, *I pick out, choose*

ἐκλεκτός, -ή, -όν, *chosen, elect*

ἐκλογή, -ῆς, ἡ, *a choosing out, election* (in the New Testament
      always of the divine choice)

διαλογίζομαι, *I debate*

root ΛΕΓ (2), say

λέγω, *I say, speak*

λόγος, -ου, ὁ, *a word, the Word*

εὐλογέω, *(I speak well of someone), I bless*

εὐλογητός, -όν, *blessed*

εὐλογία, -ας, ἡ, *a blessing*

ἀπολογέομαι, *I defend myself*

ἀπολογία, -ας, ἡ, *a defense* (especially in a law court)

λογίζομαι, *I account, reckon*

διαλογίζομαι, I debate

διαλογισμός, -οῦ, ὁ, a reasoning, questioning

root ΛΥ, loose

λύω, I loose

ἀπολύω, I release (loose from)

ἀπολύτρωσις, -εως, ἡ, (a releasing), redemption

ἐκλύομαι, I am unstrung, grow weary, become faint-hearted

καταλύω, (I dissolve), I destroy; I lodge (after having loosed
the straps and packs of the beasts of burden as well as
one's own garments)

παραλύομαι, (I am unstrung), I am a paralytic

παραλυτικός, -ή, -όν, paralytic

root ΜΑ, reflex thought, persistency

μένω, (I bethink myself, wait), I remain

διαμένω, I remain throughout

ἐπιμένω, I remain in

προσμένω, I remain with, continue in

ὑπομένω, I tarry; I endure

ὑπομονή, -ῆς, ἡ, patient, steadfast endurance

μιμητής, -οῦ, ὁ, an imitator

μιμνήσκομαι, I remember

ἀναμιμνήσκομαι, I call to remembrance

ὑπομιμνήσκω, I bring to remembrance

μνεία, -ας, ἡ, remembrance, mention

μνῆμα, -ατος, τό, (something that brings to remembrance), a
sepulcher, tomb, monument

μνημεῖον, -ου, τό, a sepulcher, tomb, monument

μνημονεύω, I remember

root MAP, thoughtful

μάρτυς, -υρος, ὁ and ἡ, a witness

μαρτυρέω, I bear witness, testify

μαρτυρία, -ας, ἡ, testimony, evidence

μαρτύριον, -ου, τό, a testimony, witness, proof

διαμαρτυρέομαι, I testify (solemnly)

root MEP, part

μέρος, -ους, τό, a part

μερίζω, I divide (make parts of)

διαμερίζω, I divide, distribute

ἁμαρτάνω, (I am without a share or part in; miss the mark),
        I sin, commit a sin

ἁμάρτημα, -ατος, τό, a sin, evil deed

ἁμαρτία, -ας, ἡ, a sin, sin

ἁμαρτωλός, -όν, sinful; as a noun, a sinner

root NEM, allot

νόμος, -ου, ὁ, a law, the Law

ἀνομία, -ας, ἡ, (without law), lawlessness

νομίζω, I suppose, think

νομικός, -ή, -όν, relating to law; as a noun, one learned in
        the (Mosaic) law, a lawyer

root NO, know

νοέω, I understand

νόημα, -ατος, τό, a thought, a design

διάνοια, -ας, ἡ, the mind, understanding, a thought

κατανοέω, I observe

μετανοέω, I repent

μετάνοια, -ας, ἡ, repentance

νοῦς, νοός, ὁ, the mind

νουθετέω, (I put in mind), I admonish, warn, exhort

οἶκος, -ου, ὁ, a house

οἰκοδεσπότης, -ου, ὁ, a householder

οἰκοδομέω, I build, edify

οἰκοδομή, -ῆς, ἡ, a building; edification

ἐποικοδομέω, I build upon, build up

οἰκονόμος, -ου, ὁ, a steward

οἰκέω, I dwell, inhabit

ἐνοικέω, I dwell in

κατοικέω, I inhabit, dwell

οἰκονομία, -ας, ἡ, stewardship, arrangement, dispensation

οἰκουμένη, -ης, ἡ, the (inhabited) world

οἰκία, -ας, ἡ, a house

root OM, like

ὅμοιος, -α, -ον, like

ὁμοιόω, I make like, liken

ὁμοίωμα, -ατος, τό, a likeness, image

ὁμολογέω, (I say the same thing), I confess, profess

ἐξομολογέομαι, I confess, profess

ὁμολογία, -ας, ἡ, a confession, profession

root ΟΠ, see

ὄψομαι, (ὄπ-σο-μαι), I shall see

ὀφθαλμός, -οῦ, ὁ, an eye

ἄνθρωπος, -ου, ὁ, ('man-faced,' cf. ἀνήρ, ἀνδρός), a man

ἀνθρώπινος, -η, -ον, human

μέτωπον, -ου, τό, forehead

πρόσωπον, -ου, τό, face

πάσχω, I suffer (2nd aor., ἔ-παθ-ον)

πάθημα, -ατος, τό, suffering

πενθέω, I mourn

παῖς, παιδός, ὁ and ἡ, a boy, girl, child, servant

παιδεύω, I teach, chastise

παιδεία, -ας, ἡ, discipline, chastisement

παιδίον, -ου, τό, an infant, child

παιδίσκη, -ης, ἡ, a maid servant

ἐμπαίζω, I mock

πᾶς, πᾶσα, πᾶν, every, all

ἅπας, -απα, -αν, (used by some authors in preference to πᾶς
     after a consonant), all

πανταχοῦ, everywhere

πάντως, entirely, assuredly

παντοκράτωρ, -ορος, ὁ, ruler of all, the Almighty

root ΠΕΡ (1), press or drive through

πορεύομαι, I go, proceed

διαπορεύομαι, I go through

εἰσπορεύομαι, I enter

ἐκπορεύομαι, I go out

παραπορεύομαι, I go past, pass by

ἔμπορος, -ου, ὁ, (one on a journey, especially for business),
     a merchant

πέραν, beyond (on the further side)

διαπεράω, I cross over

ἀπορέω, (I lose the way), I am in doubt, perplexed

πειράζω, I test, tempt, attempt

πειρασμός, -οῦ, ὁ, a temptation

root ΠΕΡ (2), causal of ΠΕΡ (1), export for sale

πιπράσκω, (for reduplicated πι-περ-ασκω), I sell

πορνεύω, I commit fornication; metaphorically of idolatry (in accord with Biblical imagery, the marriage relationship between God and his people is broken by the worship of idols)

πορνεία, -ας, ἡ, fornication

πόρνη, -ης, ἡ, (one whose body is sold), a prostitute, harlot

πόρνος, -ου, ὁ, a fornicator

root ΠΕΤ, fly, fall

πέτομαι, I fly

πετεινά, -ῶν, τά, birds

καταπέτασμα, -ατος, τό, a veil (spread out), a curtain

πίπτω, (for reduplicated πι-πετ-ω), I fall

ἀναπίπτω, I recline

ἐκπίπτω, I fall away

ἐμπίπτω, I fall into

ἐπιπίπτω, I fall upon

προσπίπτω, I fall towards, prostrate myself before

πτέρυξ, -υγος, ἡ, a wing

πτῶμα, -ατος, τό, (the fallen body of one dead), a corpse

παράπτωμα, -ατος, τό, (a fall beside), a sin, trespass

root ΠΙ and ΠΟ, drink

πίνω, I drink

καταπίνω, I drink down, devour, swallow up

ποτήριον, -ου, τό, a cup

ποτίζω, I give drink to

root ΠΙΘ, bind

πείθω, I persuade (bind myself)

ἀπειθέω, I disbelieve, disobey (not to let myself be bound)

ἀπείθεια, -ας, ἡ, disobedience, rebellion

ἀπειθής, -ές, disobedient

πεποίθησις, -εως, ἡ, trust, confidence

πίστις, -εως, ἡ, faith, belief, trust

πιστός, -ή, -όν, faithful, believing

ἄπιστος, -ον, unbelieving, faithless

ἀπιστία, -ας, ἡ, unbelief

ὀλιγόπιστος, -ον, of little faith

πιστεύω, I have faith (in), believe

ἀπιστέω, I am unfaithful, disbelieve

root ΠΛΑ, fill

πίμπλημι, I fill

ἐμπίπλημι and ἐμπιπλάω, I fill up

πλήρης, -ες, full

πληρόω, I fill, fulfill

ἀναπληρόω, I fill up

πλήρωμα, -ατος, τό, fullness

πλῆθος, -ους, τό, a multitude

πληθύνω, I multiply

πλοῦτος, -ου, ὁ, (fullness), wealth

πλούσιος, -α, -ον, rich

πλουτέω, I am rich

πλήν, (originally 'more than'), however, except

πολύς, πολλή, πολύ, much, plural many

πλείων, -ον, larger, more

πλεονάζω, I abound in, make to abound

πλεονεκτέω, (I have more), I gain the advantage of, defraud

πλεονεξία, -ας, ἡ, greedy desire to have more, covetousness

root ΣΑϜ, safe and sound, alive and well

σώζω, I save

διασώζω, I save (rescue) through (some danger)

σωτήρ, -ῆρος, ὁ, a savior, rescuer, preserver, the Saviour

σωτηρία, -ας, ἡ, salvation

σωφρονέω, I am sober-minded, self-controlled

(σθένος, -ους, τό, strength, might [not in the New Testament])

ἀσθενής, -ες, weak

ἀσθενέω, I am weak

ἀσθένεια, -ας, ἡ, lack of strength, weakness, illness

root ΣΚΑ, cover, darken

σκηνή, -ῆς, ἡ, a tent, tabernacle

σκηνόω, I dwell in a tent, encamp

σκιά, -ᾶς, ἡ, a shadow

ἐπισκιάζω, I overshadow, envelop

σκότος, -ους, τό, darkness

σκοτία, -ας, ἡ, darkness

σκοτίζομαι, I am covered with darkness, darkened

root ΣΤΑ, stand, set

ἵστημι, I cause to stand; I stand

ἀνθίστημι, (I stand against), I resist

ἀνίστημι, I cause to rise; I arise

ἀφίστημι, I withdraw, depart

ἐνίστημι, I am at hand, am present

ἐξίστημι, (I set out of one's senses), I amaze, am amazed

ἐφίστημι, I stand over, come upon

ἐπιστάτης, -ου, ὁ, (one standing over another), a master (found
   only in Luke, used of Jesus)

ἐπίσταμαι, I understand, know

καθίστημι, I set, constitute

ἀποκαθίστημι and ἀποκαθιστάνω, I set up again, restore to its
   former state

μεθίστημι and μεθιστάνω, I transfer, remove

παρίστημι, I am present, stand by

προΐστημι, I stand in front, lead, rule, practice

συνίστημι and συνιστάνω, I commend; I stand with, consist

στάσις, -εως, ἡ, a standing, an insurrection

ἀνάστασις, -εως, ἡ, (a standing up), resurrection

ἔκστασις, -εως, ἡ, (standing outside oneself), bewilderment, a
   trance

ὑπόστασις, -εως, ἡ, (a standing under), substance, confidence

ἀκαταστασία, -ας, ἡ, instability, disturbance, revolution

root ΣΤΑΥ or ΣΤΑϜ, lengthened form of ΣΤΑ

σταυρός, -οῦ, ὁ, a cross

σταυρόω, I crucify

συνσταυρόω, I crucify along with

root ΣΤΕΛ, set in order, equip

ἀποστέλλω, I send away (with a commission)

ἀπόστολος, -ου, ὁ, an Apostle

διαστέλλομαι, I command, charge expressly

ἐξαποστέλλω, I send forth

ἐπιστολή, -ῆς, ἡ, (thing sent by a messenger), a letter

στολή, -ῆς, ἡ, (a piece of equipment, especially of clothes,
      apparel), a long robe, a festal robe

root ΣΤΡΕΦ, turn

στρέφω, I turn

ἀναστρέφω, I return; I live

ἀναστροφή, -ῆς, ἡ, conduct

διαστρέφω, I pervert

ἐπιστρέφω, I turn to, return

ὑποστρέφω, I return

root ΤΑΓ, arrange, order

τάσσω, I arrange, appoint, order

ἀντιτάσσομαι, I range in battle against, resist

ἀποτάσσομαι, I separate myself, take leave of, forsake

διατάσσω, I command

ἐπιτάσσω, I command

ἐπιταγή, -ῆς, ἡ, a command, order, authority

ὑποτάσσω, I subject

τάξις, -εως, ἡ, an arrangement, order, right order, office

root ΤΕΛ, end

τέλος, -ους, τό, end

τελέω, I finish, fulfill

ἐπιτελέω, I complete, perform

συντελέω, I finish, accomplish

συντέλεια, -ας, ἡ, completion, consummation

τέλειος, -α, -ον, complete, perfect, mature

τελειόω, I complete, make perfect

τελευτάω, (I come to the end of life), I die

τέσσαρες, -αρα, four

δεκατέσσαρες, -αρα, fourteen

τεσσαράκοντα, indeclinable, forty

τέταρτος, -η, -ον, fourth

τράπεζα, -ης, ἡ, (four-footed), a table

root TI, honor, pay

τιμή, -ῆς, ἡ, honor, price

τιμάω, I honor

ἐπιτιμάω, I rebuke, warn

τίμιος, -α, -ον, honorable, precious

ἀτιμάζω, I dishonor, insult

ἀτιμία, -ας, ἡ, dishonor, disgrace

ἔντιμος, -ον, held in honor, precious, prized

τρεῖς, τρία, three

τριάκοντα, indeclinable, thirty

τρίτος, -η, -ον, third

τρίς, thrice, three times

ὑψηλός, -ή, -όν, high

ὕψιστος, -η, -ον, highest

ὕψος, -ους, τό, height, heaven

ὑψόω, I lift up, exalt

root ΦΛΓ, ΦΑ, and ΦΑΝ, shine, show

φαίνω, I shine, appear

ἐπιφάνεια, -ας, ἡ, an appearing, manifestation (of Christ in
    glory)

ἀφανίζω, (I make unseen), I destroy; passive, I vanish

ἐμφανίζω, I manifest

φανερός, -ά, -όν, manifest

φανερόω, I make manifest

ὑπερήφανος, -ον, (showing oneself above others), haughty, dis-
    dainful

φημί, (I bring to light, make known), I say

προφητεύω, I prophesy

προφητεία, -ας, ἡ, a prophecy

προφήτης, -ου, ὁ, a prophet

φωνή, -ῆς, ἡ, a sound, voice

φωνέω, I call

συμφωνέω, I am in accord, agree with

βλασφημέω, I blaspheme

βλασφημία, -ας, ἡ, blasphemy

πρόφασις, -εως, ἡ, a pretense, pretext

φῶς, (contracted from φάος), φωτός, τό, light

φωτεινός, -ή, -όν, shining, brilliant

φωτίζω, I shed light on, enlighten

root ΦΕΡ, bear

φέρω, I carry, bear, lead

ἀποφέρω, I carry off, bear away

διαφέρω, (I bear apart), I differ

εἰσφέρω, I bring in, into

ἐκφέρω, I carry out, bring out

προσφέρω, I bring to, offer

προσφορά, -ᾶς, ἡ, an offering, a sacrifice

συμφέρω, I bring together; it is profitable

φορέω, I bear, carry, wear

καρποφορέω, I bear fruit

πληροφορέω, I accomplish, satisfy fully, fully convince

φορτίον, -ου, τό, a burden, load

root ΦΡΕΝ (in φρήν, midriff, heart, mind)

φρονέω, I think

καταφρονέω, I despise, scorn

σωφρονέω, I am sober minded, self-controlled

ταπεινοφροσύνη, -ης, ἡ, lowliness of mind, humility

φρόνιμος, -η, -ον, *prudent*
ἄφρων, -ον, *foolish*
εὐφραίνω, *I rejoice*

root ΦΥ, bring forth

φυλή, -ῆς, ἡ, *a tribe*
φύλλον, -ου, τό, *a leaf*
φύσις, -εως, ἡ, *nature*
φυτεύω, *I plant*

root ΧΑΡ, rejoice

χαίρω, *I rejoice* (2nd aor. pass. ἐ-χάρ-ην)
συνχαίρω, *I rejoice with*
χαρά, -ᾶς, ἡ, *joy, delight*
χάρις, -ιτος, ἡ, *grace, favor*
χάριν, (accusative of the noun χάρις used absolutely, *in favor
of, for the pleasure of*), preposition with the gen., *on
account of, for the sake of*
χαρίζομαι, *I give freely, forgive*
χάρισμα, -ατος, τό, *a free (gracious) gift*
εὐχαριστέω, *I give thanks*
εὐχαριστία, -ας, ἡ, *thanksgiving*

χιλιάς, -άδος, ἡ, *a thousand*
χίλιοι, -αι, -α, *a thousand*
χιλίαρχος, -ου, ὁ, *a military tribune, captain*
τετρακισχίλιοι, -αι, -α, *four thousand*
πεντακισχίλιοι, -αι, -α, *five thousand*

χράομαι, *I use*

χρεία, -ας, ἡ, a need

χρηστός, -ή, -όν, (useful, good), mild, comfortable, gracious

χρηστότης, -ητος, ἡ, goodness, kindness

χρῄζω, I have need of

χρῆμα, -ατος, τό, (whatever one uses, a thing), money; plural, riches

χρηματίζω, (I transact business, hence, consult, deliberate), I make answer (in an oracle), I warn; passive, I am warned by God; I receive a name (from my business), am called _____

χρυσός, -οῦ, ὁ, gold

χρυσίον, -ου, τό, gold

χρύσεος, -α, -ον, contracted χρυσοῦς, -ῆ, -οῦν, golden _____

χώρα, -ας, ἡ, a country

χωρίον, -ου, τό, a place, field

χωρέω, I make room, hold

ἀναχωρέω, I depart

χωρίζω, I separate, depart _____

ψεύδομαι, I lie

ψευδομαρτυρέω, I testify falsely, bear false witness

ψευδοπροφήτης, -ου, ὁ, a false prophet

ψεῦδος, -ους, τό, a lie

ψεύστης, -ου, ὁ, a liar

THE INDO—EUROPEAN FAMILY OF LANGUAGES

Languages, like individuals, are related to each other in families. According to one estimate there have been approximately 2796 languages in the world and these may be classified into about 26 families.[1] The family which interests the student of New Testament Greek is that which scholars have named the Indo-European family. Besides Greek this family includes seven other sub-families of languages, the Indo-Iranian, Armenian, Albanian, Italic, Celtic, Germanic, and Balto-Slavic. (See Table I on pp. 96f.)

What region was the common center, the home of the parent tongue from which these Indo-European languages have developed, has been a notorious subject of discussion.[2] Earlier investigators were quite confident that it was in Asia — the continent which was the source of the oldest civilization, the traditional site of the Garden of Eden, and the locality where Sanskrit was spoken. But more recently certain scholars have favored the hypothesis that localizes what is popularly called 'the cradle of the Aryans' in the region extending north of the Black Sea and Caucasia, and south and west of the Volga River.[3]

Beginning about 3000 B.C. it is probable that successive migrations of tribes left the old home and drifted, some south-

[1] Louis H. Gray, *Foundations of Language* (New York, 1939), pp. 417f and 303.

[2] The question has not yet been satisfactorily answered. One of the most recent significant discussions is F. Specht's 'Sprachliches zur Urheimat der Indogermanen' in Kuhn's *Zeitschrift für vergleichende Sprachforschung*, LXVI (1939), pp. 1-74. Further bibliography may be found in Gray, *op. cit.*, pp. 457f.

[3] See, e.g., Harold H. Bender, *The Home of the Indo-Europeans* (Princeton, 1922), and Gray, *op. cit.*, pp. 304-310.

TABLE I   THE INDO-EUROPEAN LANGUAGES

Extant modern languages are in the last column.

INDO-IRANIAN	Indic	Vedic Sanskrit; Classical Sanskrit	Pāli, Prakrit dialects	Bengali Hindi Marathi Gujerati etc.
	Iranian	Avestan Old Persian	Pahlavi Sogdian Sacian	Mod. Persian Kurdish Ossetan Afghan Baluchi etc.
ARMENIAN			Old Armenian	Armenian
ALBANIAN				Albanian
GREEK	East Greek	Attic-Ionic Arcadian-Cyprian Aeolic: Lesbian, Thessalian, Boeotian	The *koine* or Hellenistic Greek	Mod. Greek
	West Greek	NW Greek: Locrian, Phocian, Elean Doric: Laconian, Argolic, Corinthian Cretan, etc		(Tsaconian dialect)
ITALIC	Latin-Faliscan	Latin Faliscan	Vulgar Latin	French Provençal Catalan Spanish Portuguese Italian Rhaeto-Roman Rumanian
	Oscan-Umbrian	Oscan Umbrian Paelignian Volscian, etc.		

Table I, continued

CELTIC	Gaelic		Old Irish	Irish Scotch Gaelic Manx
	Britannic		Old Welsh Old Cornish Old Breton	Welsh Breton
	Continental	Celtic Inscriptions		
GERMANIC	East Germanic		Gothic	
	North Germanic		Old Norse	Swedish Danish Norwegian Icelandic
	West Germanic	Anglo-Frisian	Old English Old Frisian	English Frisian
		German — Low / High	Old Saxon Old Low Franconian Old High German	Dutch German
BALTO-SLAVIC	Baltic		Old Lithuanian Old Lettic Old Prussian	Lithuanian Lettic
	Slavic	South Slavic	Old Church Slavic	Bulgarian Serbo-Croatian Slovenian
		West Slavic	Polabian	Bohemian Slovak Polish Wendish
		East Slavic		Great Russian White Russian Ukrainian

——From Carl D. Buck, *Comparative Grammar of Greek and Latin* (2nd impression, Chicago, 1937), pp. 3f.

Tocharian and Hittite likewise belong to the Indo-European family but their exact relationships have not yet been fully determined.

east to the Ganges valley, others westward throughout Europe.[4]
No remains of the parent Indo-European tongue are extant, but,
by means of comparative linguistics, scholars have been able to
reconstruct a large part of its vocabulary and grammar.[5]

The method and validity of comparative linguistics can be
illustrated within one branch of the Indo-European family. The
Romance languages are obviously related because it can be observed that, within historic times, they have assumed their
present forms in developing from their common source, the Latin
language. Thus, for example, the Latin word *caballus*, meaning
'a pack-horse, a nag,' is the origin of all Romance words for
'horse,' such as French *cheval*, Spanish *caballo*, Italian *cavallo*, Portuguese *cavallo*, Rumanian *cal*, Provençal and Catalan,
cavall.[6] So, too, when various extant Indo-European languages
are compared, the hypothetical parent tongue may be reconstruc-
ted with a considerable degree of probability. Thus, the fact
that the Greek word μήτηρ resembles the Sanskrit *mātár-*, Aves-
tan (Old Persian) *mātā*, Old Armenian *mair*, Latin *māter*, Old High
German *muoter* (modern German *Mutter*), Old Irish *māthir*, Old
Slavic *mati*, etc., renders it highly probable that all these
words have come from an Indo-European word **mātér-*.[7]

---

[4] Today all of the languages of Europe belong to the Indo-European
family except Basque, Esthonian, Finnish, Hungarian, Lapp, and Turkish.

[5] The most recent works of this kind are A. Walde and J. Pokorny,
Etymologisches Wörterbuch der indogermanischen Sprachen (3 vols., Berlin
and Leipzig, 1930-32), A. Meillet, *Introduction à l'étude comparative
des langues indo-européenes* (7th ed., Paris, 1934), and H. Hirt, *Indo-
germanische Grammatik* (7 vols., Heidelberg, 1921-37).

[6] For still other dialectical forms, see W. Meyer-Lübke, *Roman-
isches etymologisches Wörterbuch* (3rd ed., Heidelberg, 1930), s.v. *caballus*.

[7] The asterisk signifies that this word does not appear in any
historical source. For other derivations from this stem, see Walde-
Pokorny, *op. cit.*, s.v., *mātér-*.

The words for 'horse' in the Romance languages, all of
which have originated from the same Latin word, are said to be
cognate to one another. So, too, besides words in English which
are borrowed or derived from Greek (such as the derivatives supplied in Part I), other English words are said to be cognate to
words in Greek. Cognate words, as their name indicates,[8] are
words, in different languages, which are 'related' to each other
because they have descended from the same ancestor. Though Greek
and English have been separated from their common parent stock
for so many centuries and have become widely different in so
many respects, linguists have observed that some of the differ-
ences can be accounted for in terms of regular phonetic changes.
Thus, because Greek and English are sister languages, it is
possible to identify words in each which have descended from
the same words in the primitive Indo-European speech. Jacob
Grimm (1785-1863) formulated a statement of the mutation of
consonants involved in the development of the Teutonic languages.[9]
(In all languages consonants are the skeleton-letters of words,
for vowel-sounds are far from being as persistent — a fact
which may be observed by noting the differing local pronuncia-
tions of the same words in our own language.)[10]

How Grimm's law operates is shown in the following table,
which indicates what forms the consonants in the Greek group
will assume in the English group, and illustrates them by a few
examples. The Greek declensional terminations have, of course,

[8] Latin *cognatus*, 'related (by blood).'

[9] For a most interesting account of the steps by which the present
formulation of Grimm's law was attained, see Leonard Bloomfield's book
entitled *Language* (New York, 1933), pp. 14f and 347-359.

[10] E.g., a man wears a 'doiby' hat in the Bronx, a 'darby' in Great
Britain, and a 'derby' elsewhere.

no correspondence in the English words. Other words which might be thought to be exceptions to Grimm's law are accounted for by Grassmann's law and Verner's law.[11]

The consonants which are involved are those that form the so-called square of mutes:

	voiceless	voiced	aspirate
Labials (lip sounds)	π	β	φ
Dentals (teeth sounds)	τ	δ	θ
Palatals (palate sounds)	κ	γ	χ

1. The voiceless stops, π, τ, κ, are represented in cognate English words by *f*, *th*, *h*.

(a) π and *f* — English cognate

πατήρ 'father' — *f*ather

πληγή 'stroke, blow' — *f*lick, *f*log

πολύς 'much' — *f*ull, *f*ill

πούς 'foot' — *f*oot

πῦρ 'fire' — *f*ire

(b) τ and *th*

ὀδούς (stem ὀδόντ-) 'tooth' — too*th*

τρεῖς 'three' — *th*ree

(c) κ and *h*

καρδία 'heart' — *h*eart

καρπός 'fruit' — *h*arvest

κύων (stem κυν-) 'dog' — *h*ound

2. The voiced stops, β, δ, γ, are represented in cognate English words by *p*, *t*, *k*.

[11] A succinct statement of these laws may be read in Webster's *New International Dictionary*, 2nd ed., s.vv.

(a) β and *p*   English cognate

    βύρσα 'a hide'   *p*urse

    κύβος 'loin'   hi*p*

(b) δ and *t*

    δρῦς 'oak'   *t*ree

    δύο 'two'   *t*wo

    ὀδόντ- 'tooth'   *t*ooth

(c) γ and *k*

    γένος 'race, family'   *k*in

    γόνυ 'knee'   *k*nee

    γινώσκω (stem γνω-) 'know'   *k*now

3. The aspirated stops, φ, θ, χ, are represented in cognate
English words by *b*, *d*, *g*.

(a) φ and *b*   English cognate

    φέρω 'I bear'   *b*ear

    φράτηρ 'a member of a

                 brotherhood'   *b*rother

(b) θ and *d*

    θυγάτηρ 'daughter'   *d*aughter

    θύρα 'door'   *d*oor

    μέθυ 'wine'   mea*d*

    τίθημι (stem θε-) 'I put,

                   place'   *d*o

(c) χ and *g*

    ὀχέω 'I uphold, carry,

                   ride'   wei*g*h

    χήν (dat. plu. χησί) 'goose'   *g*oose

    χόρτος 'enclosure, grass'   *g*arden

APPENDIX II

PREPOSITIONS IN COMPOSITION WITH VERBS

Originally a preposition was an auxiliary word which assisted in defining and clarifying the significance of the case of a noun.[1] When a preposition is compounded with a verb its primitive connotation may acquire various other functions and meanings. One of the most important of these is the so-called 'perfective' use of the preposition. When used in this way the preposition usually completes or emphasizes the action conveyed by the simple verb. All Indo-European languages employ prepositions in this perfectivizing sense. Compare, for example, the English verbs *bring* and *bring up*, *burn* and *burn up*, *carry* and *carry off*, *drink* and *drink up*, *eat* and *eat up*, *follow* and *follow up* or *follow through*, *go* and *go away*, *knock* and *knock down*, *make* and *make over*, *pluck* and *pluck out*, *speak* and *speak out*, *wake* and *wake up*, *work* and *work out*. In each instance the compound verb intensifies the sense of the simple verb. So too in Greek— although Greek and English do not always use the same preposition to convey the same idea. Compare ἐργάζομαι, *I work*, with κατεργάζομαι, *I work out* (literally *down to the finish,* see Phil. 2:12); καίομαι, *I burn*, with κατακαίομαι, *I burn up, burn completely* (see Matt. 3:12); ἐσθίω, *I eat*, with κατεσθίω, *I eat up, devour* (see Luke 20:47).[2]

[1] See, further, A.T. Robertson, *A Grammar of the Greek New Testament in the Light of Historical Research* (5th ed., New York, 1931), pp. 553-557. The primary meanings of Greek prepositions used with various cases may be seen in Table II on p. 103.

[2] For additional information about perfective verbs see J.H. Moulton, *A Grammar of New Testament Greek*, vol. I, *Prolegomena*, (3rd ed., Edinburgh, 1908), pp. 111-118.

TABLE II GEOMETRIC ARRANGEMENT OF THE GREEK PREPOSITIONS

15 ἀντί G over against

16 πρό G before

17 ὀπίσω G behind, after

11 περί A around

1 ὑπέρ A above

18 σύν D with

19 μετά G with
   A after

10 ἀπό G
   away from

14 κατά G
   down

9 ἐκ G
   out of

2 ἐπί G upon;

8 ἐν D in

3 ὑπό A under

4 παρά D A beside

5 ἀμφί- on both sides of

7 εἰς A into

12 διά G through

6 πρός A towards

13 ἀνά A up

Notes: 1. The symbols G, D, and A should be read: "with the genitive case means," "with the dative case means," and "with the accusative case means." Number 5 appears in the New Testament only in compound words.

2. Only the basic meanings of prepositions with certain cases are given here. For other meanings with other cases, a lexicon should be consulted.

In the following list each preposition is analyzed as to its principal meanings when in composition with verbs. Most of the semantic shifts are perfectly clear. Occasionally, however, the meaning of the compound verb cannot easily be determined from the separate meanings of its component parts. Thus, the force of ἀπό in ἀποκρίνομαι and in ἀποθνήσκω is no longer obvious. Perhaps originally the former verb meant 'I answer *back*' and the latter 'I die *off*.'

It will be remembered that a preposition which ends in a vowel drops that vowel when compounded with a verb which begins with a vowel, as ἀπέρχομαι from ἀπό and ἔρχομαι. The only exceptions to this rule are compounds with περί and πρό, which do not drop their final vowel, as προάγω and περιάγω.

ἀνά (1) Root meaning *upwards*
      ἀναβαίνω, I *go up*
      ἀνίστημι, I *cause to stand up*
  (2) *Again, anew, thoroughly*
      ἀναζάω, I *live again, revive*
      ἀναπαύω, I *give rest to* (someone) *thoroughly, refresh*
      ἀνασταυρόω, I *crucify afresh*
  (3) *Back, backwards, to and fro*
      ἀναστρέφω, I *turn upside down, turn back, walk to and*
          fro, conduct myself, live
      ἀναστροφή, '*walk*,' *conduct*

ἀντί (1) Root meaning *opposite, against, over against*
      ἀντιπαρέρχομαι, I *pass by* [παρά] *on the other side*
      ἀντιλέγω, I *speak against, oppose, resist*
      ἀντίχριστος, *an opponent of Christ, antichrist*

(2) *Requital*

ἀνταποδίδωμι, *I give back as an equivalent, recompense or requital* (ἀντί expresses the idea of a full, complete return)

ἀντιμισθία, *reward, requital*

(3) *Substitution*

ἀνθύπατος (ἀντί and ὕπατος, an alternative form of ὑπέρτατος, *supreme*), *a proconsul*

Perhaps ἀντίχριστος should be classified here as 'one who assumes the guise of Christ (in order to seduce His people)'

ἀπό (1) Root meaning *away from*

ἀπέρχομαι, *I depart from*

ἀποκαλύπτω, *I withdraw a cover from, uncover, reveal*

(2) *Back again* (like Latin re-)

ἀποδίδωμι, *I give back, return*

ἀπολαμβάνω, *I take back, recover*

(3) *Perfective*

ἀπέχω, *I have fully, have received* (in full), see Matt. 6:2, 5, 16; also in sense (1), *I am away, distant;* middle, *I hold myself off from, abstain*

ἀπόλλυμι, *I destroy utterly;* middle, *I perish completely*

ἀπολούομαι, *I wash off myself thoroughly*

διά (1) Root meaning *through*

διέρχομαι, *I go through, pass through*

(2) *Distribution*

διαγγέλλω, *I publish abroad, proclaim*

διαδίδωμι, *I distribute*

    (3) *Transition, change*

        διαβάλλω, *I throw across, slander*

        διαλλάσσω, *I change* (make other [ἄλλος] than), *recon-*
          cile

    (4) *Separation*

        διασπάω, *I tear apart*

    (5) *Perfective*

        διαβεβαιόομαι, *I assert confidently, emphatically*

        διακαθαρίζω, *I cleanse thoroughly*

        διαφυλάσσω, *I guard carefully*

εἰς Root meaning *into*

        εἰσέρχομαι, *I go into, enter*

ἐκ   (1) Root meaning *from out of*

        ἐκβάλλω, *I cast out*

        ἐξέρχομαι, *I go out*

    (2) *Perfective*

        ἐκπληρόω, *I fill completely*

        ἐξαπορέομαι, *I am utterly at a loss*

ἐν   (1) Root meaning *in*

        ἐνοικέω, *I dwell in*

    (2) Motion *into*

        ἐμβαίνω, *I step into* [a boat], *I embark*

ἐπί (1) Root meaning *on, upon*

        ἐπιβάλλω, *I cast, lay,* or *put upon*

        ἐπιτίθημι, *I lay, set,* or *place upon*

    (2) Motion *towards*

ἐπέρχομαι, *I come upon* (sometimes with hostility)

ἐπιβάλλω, *I lay or put upon*

(3) *Upwards*

ἐπαίρω, *I lift up, raise*

(4) *Superintendence*

ἐπίσκοπος, *one who oversees, a bishop*

ἐπιστάτης, *one who is set over, a master*

κατά (1) Root meaning *down from, down*

καταβαίνω, *I go down*

(2) *Opposition*

κατακρίνω, *I give judgment against, condemn*

καταράομαι, *I pray against, curse*

(3) *In succession, in order*

καταρτίζω, *I set in order, mend*

κατευθύνω, *I make straight, guide, direct*

(4) *After, behind*

κατακολουθέω, *I follow after*

καταλείπω, *I leave behind, forsake*

(5) *Perfective*

κατεργάζομαι, *I work out thoroughly, accomplish*

κατεσθίω, *I eat up, devour*

μετά (1) Root meaning *association with*

μεταδίδωμι, *I share* (a thing) *with* (anyone), *impart*

μετέχω, *I partake of, share in*

(2) *Change, alteration*

μεταβαίνω, *I pass from one place to another, depart*

μεταμορφόω, *I change to another form, transform, trans-*
    figure

μετανοέω, I change my mind or purpose, repent

(3) After, in search of

μεταπέμπω, I send after or for, summon

παρά (1) Root meaning beside, near

παραγίνομαι, I am at hand, arrive

παρακαλέω, I call to my side, summon, admonish, entreat, encourage, comfort

(2) Violation, transgression, neglect

παραβαίνω, I go by the side of (and beyond), overstep, transgress

παρακούω, I hear amiss, hear without heeding, disobey

περί (1) Root meaning in a circuit about, around

περιβάλλω, I throw around, I clothe

περιπατέω, I walk about, Hebraistically, in an ethical sense, I conduct myself, live

(2) Beyond (because that which surrounds a thing does not belong to the thing itself but is beyond it)

περισσεύω, I exceed (the ordinary, the necessary), I abound, cause to abound

πρό Root meaning before (of place or time), forth

προάγω, I lead forth, go before

προγινώσκω, I know beforehand, foreknow

προφητεύω, I foretell, speak forth, prophesy

πρός (1) Root meaning to, towards

προσέρχομαι, I come to, approach

προσέχω, I bring to; with τὸν νοῦν, I turn the mind to,

attend to, give heed to myself, beware

προσκυνέω, I kiss the hand to (towards) one (in token
of reverence), fall down before, worship

(2) On, at

προσκόπτω, I strike (the hand or foot) against, stumble
at

σύν (1) Root meaning together with

συνάγω, I gather together

συνεργέω, I work together

συνίημι, (I bring together in the mind), I understand

(2) Perfective

συνθρύπτω, I break in pieces, crush utterly

συνκαλύπτω, I veil (cover) completely

συντηρέω, I keep safe

ὑπέρ Root meaning over, above

ὑπερβάλλω, (I throw over or beyond), I exceed, surpass

ὑπερέχω, (I have or hold over), I am superior, excel

ὑπερνικάω, I am more than a conqueror

ὑπό Root meaning under, hence of subjection and compliance

ὑποδέομαι, I bind under (the foot)

ὑπομένω, (I remain under), I remain, persevere, endure

ὑπάγω, (I lead under), I withdraw myself, depart

APPENDIX III   TABLE OF CORRELATIVE PRONOUNS AND ADVERBS

	DEMONSTRATIVE	INTERROGATIVE	INDEFINITE	RELATIVE and/or INDEFINITE RELATIVE
SIMPLE	ὅδε, this (here) οὗτος, this (near) ἐκεῖνος, that (yonder)	τίς; who? which? what?	τις, someone, anyone	ὅς, who, which ὅστις, whoever, whichever
PLACE	αὐτοῦ, there, here ὧδε, hither, here	ποῦ; where?	ποῦ, somewhere	οὗ, where, whither ὅπου, where, whither
	ἐντεῦθεν, hence ἐκεῖθεν, thence	πόθεν; whence?		ὅθεν, whence
	ἐκεῖ, there ἐνθάδε, here, hither			
MANNER	οὕτως, thus, so	πῶς; how?	πώς, at all, somehow, in any way	ὡς, as, as, about
TIME	νῦν and νυνί, now τότε, then	πότε; when?	ποτέ, at some time, once, ever	ὅτε, when ὅταν, whenever, when
QUANTITY	τοσοῦτος, so great, so much	πόσος; how great? how much?		ὅσος, as great as, as much as
QUALITY	τοιοῦτος, of such a kind, such	ποῖος; of what sort? what?		οἷος, such as ὁποῖος, of what sort
SIZE	τηλικοῦτος, so large, so great	πηλίκος; how large? how great?		ἡλίκος, what size of

PRINCIPAL PARTS OF SOME IMPORTANT VERBS

The following list of principal parts is a summary of some of the important verbs in the New Testament. The seven irregular verbs which are given above on pages 60-61 have not been repeated here. The enclosing of a principal part in parentheses signifies that no form of the tense system immediately derived from that part occurs in the New Testament. In some instances, however, compound verbs which involve that principal part are found in the New Testament. It will be understood that, because of the exigencies of space, the definitions of these verbs have been severely limited.

PRESENT	FUTURE	AORIST	PERFECT ACTIVE	PERFECT MIDDLE	AORIST PASSIVE
ἀγαπάω *love*	ἀγαπήσω	ἠγάπησα	ἠγάπηκα.	ἠγάπημαι	ἠγαπήθην
ἄγω *lead*	ἄξω	ἤγαγον ἦξα	(ἦχα)	ἦγμαι	ἤχθην
αἴρω *take up, take away*	ἀρῶ	ἦρα	ἦρκα	ἦρμαι	ἤρθην
αἰτέω *ask for*	αἰτήσω	ᾔτησα	ᾔτηκα	(ᾔτημαι)	ᾐτήθην
ἀκούω *hear*	ἀκούσω	ἤκουσα	ἀκήκοα	(ἤκουσμαι)	ἠκούσθην
ἁμαρτάνω *sin*	ἁμαρτήσω	ἡμάρτησα ἥμαρτον	ἡμάρτηκα	(ἡμάρτημαι)	(ἡμαρτήθην)

PRESENT	FUTURE	AORIST	PERFECT ACTIVE	PERFECT MIDDLE	AORIST PASSIVE
ἀνοίγω open	ἀνοίξω	ἀνέῳξα ἤνοιξα ἤνέῳξα	ἀνέῳγα	ἀνέῳγμαι ἠνέῳγμαι ἤνοιγμαι	ἀνεῴχθην ἠνοίχθην ἠνεῴχθην
ἀπόλλυμι destroy	ἀπολέσω ἀπολῶ	ἀπώλεσα	ἀπόλωλα		
ἀποστέλλω send	ἀποστελῶ	ἀπέστειλα	ἀπέσταλκα	ἀπέσταλμαι	ἀπεστάλην
ἀφίημι let go;	ἀφήσω forgive	ἀφῆκα	ἀφεῖκα	ἀφεῖμαι	ἀφέθην
βάλλω throw	βαλῶ	ἔβαλον ἔβαλα	βέβληκα	βέβλημαι	ἐβλήθην
γεννάω beget	γεννήσω	ἐγέννησα	γεγέννηκα	γεγέννημαι	ἐγεννήθην
γίνομαι become	γενήσομαι	ἐγενόμην	γέγονα	γεγένημαι	ἐγενήθην
γινώσκω know	γνώσομαι	ἔγνων	ἔγνωκα	ἔγνωσμαι	ἐγνώσθην
γράφω write	γράψω	ἔγραψα	γέγραφα	γέγραμμαι	ἐγράφην
δείκνυμι show	δείξω	ἔδειξα	(δέδειχα)	δέδειγμαι	ἐδείχθην
δίδωμι give	δώσω	ἔδωκα	δέδωκα	δέδομαι	ἐδόθην
διώκω pursue	διώξω	ἐδίωξα	(δεδίωχα)	δεδίωγμαι	ἐδιώχθην
δοξάζω glorify	δοξάσω	ἐδόξασα	(δεδόξακα)	δεδόξασμαι	ἐδοξάσθην
ἐγείρω raise up	ἐγερῶ	ἤγειρα		ἐγήγερμαι	ἠγέρθην
ἐλέγχω convict,	ἐλέγξω reprove	ἤλεγξα			ἠλέγχθην
ἐλεέω pity	ἐλεήσω	ἠλέησα	(ἠλέηκα)	ἠλέημαι	ἠλεήθην

PRESENT	FUTURE	AORIST	PERFECT ACTIVE	PERFECT MIDDLE	AORIST PASSIVE
ἐλπίζω hope	ἐλπιῶ	ἤλπισα	ἤλπικα		
ἐρωτάω ask	ἐρωτήσω	ἠρώτησα	(ἠρώτηκα)	(ἠρώτημαι)	ἠρωτήθην
ἑτοιμάζω prepare	ἑτοιμάσω	ἡτοίμασα	ἡτοίμακα	ἡτοίμασμαι	ἡτοιμάσθην
εὐαγγελίζω preach the gospel	(εὐαγγελίσω)	εὐηγγέλισα	(εὐηγγέλικα)	εὐηγγέλισμαι	εὐηγγελίσθην
εὐλογέω bless	εὐλογήσω	εὐλόγησα	εὐλόγηκα	εὐλόγημαι	εὐλογήθην
εὑρίσκω find	εὑρήσω	εὗρον	εὕρηκα	(εὕρημαι)	εὑρέθην
ἔχω have	ἕξω	ἔσχον	ἔσχηκα		
ἥκω am come	ἥξω	ἧξα	ἧκα		
θαυμάζω marvel	θαυμάσομαι	ἐθαύμασα	(τεθαύμακα)		ἐθαυμάσθην
θεραπεύω heal	θεραπεύσω	ἐθεράπευσα	(τεθεράπευκα)	τεθεράπευμαι	ἐθεραπεύθην
θύω sacrifice		ἔθυσα		τέθυμαι	ἐτύθην
ἵστημι stand	στήσω	ἔστησα ἔστην	ἕστηκα	(ἕσταμαι)	ἐστάθην
καθαρίζω cleanse	καθαριῶ	ἐκαθάρισα		κεκαθάρισμαι	ἐκαθαρίσθην
καλέω call	καλέσω	ἐκάλεσα	κέκληκα	κέκλημαι	ἐκλήθην
κηρύσσω proclaim	κηρύξω	ἐκήρυξα	(κεκήρυχα)	(κεκήρυγμαι)	ἐκηρύχθην
κρίνω judge	κρινῶ	ἔκρινα	κέκρικα	κέκριμαι	ἐκρίθην
λαλέω speak	λαλήσω	ἐλάλησα	λελάληκα	λελάλημαι	ἐλαλήθην

PRESENT	FUTURE	AORIST	PERFECT ACTIVE	PERFECT MIDDLE	AORIST PASSIVE
λαμβάνω take	λήμψομαι	ἔλαβον	εἴληφα	εἴλημμαι	ἐλήμφθην
λείπω leave	λείψω	ἔλιπον	(λέλοιπα)	λέλειμμαι	ἐλείφθην
λύω loose	λύσω	ἔλυσα	λέλυκα	λέλυμαι	ἐλύθην
μαρτυρέω bear witness	μαρτυρήσω	ἐμαρτύρησα	μεμαρτύρηκα	μεμαρτύρημαι	ἐμαρτυρήθην
μένω remain	μενῶ	ἔμεινα	μεμένηκα		
ξηραίνω dry up		ἐξήρανα		ἐξήραμμαι	ἐξηράνθην
οἰκοδομέω build	οἰκοδομήσω	ῳκοδόμησα		ῳκοδόμημαι	ῳκοδομήθην
πάσχω suffer	(πείσομαι)	ἔπαθον	πέπονθα		
πείθω persuade	πείσω	ἔπεισα	πέποιθα	τέπεισμαι	ἐπείσθην
πειράζω tempt	(πειράσω)	ἐπείρασα	(πεπείρακα)	πεπείρασμαι	ἐπειράσθην
πέμπω send	πέμψω	ἔπεμψα	(πέπομφα)	(πέπεμμαι)	ἐπέμφθην
πίνω drink	πίομαι	ἔπιον	πέπωκα	(πέπομαι)	ἐπόθην
πίπτω fall	πεσοῦμαι	ἔπεσον ἔπεσα	πέπτωκα		
πιστεύω believe	πιστεύσω	ἐπίστευσα	πεπίστευκα	πεπίστευμαι	ἐπιστεύθην
πληρόω fill, fulfill	πληρώσω	ἐπλήρωσα	πεπλήρωκα	πεπλήρωμαι	ἐπληρώθην
ποιέω do, make	ποιήσω	ἐποίησα	πεποίηκα	πεποίημαι	(ἐποιήθην)
πράσσω do, perform	πράξω	ἔπραξα	πέπραχα	πέπραγμαι	

PRESENT	FUTURE	AORIST	PERFECT ACTIVE	PERFECT MIDDLE	AORIST PASSIVE
σπείρω sow	(σπερῶ)	ἔσπειρα		ἔσπαρμαι	ἐσπάρην
σταυρόω crucify	σταυρώσω	ἐσταύρωσα	(ἐσταύρωκα)	ἐσταύρωμαι	ἐσταυρώθην
στηρίζω strengthen	στηρίξω στηρίσω	ἐστήριξα ἐστήρισα		ἐστήριγμαι	ἐστηρίχθην
στρέφω turn	(στρέψω)	ἔστρεψα		(ἔστραμμαι)	ἐστράφην
σώζω save	σώσω	ἔσωσα	σέσωκα	σέσωσμαι σέσωμαι	ἐσώθην
τελέω finish, fulfill	(τελέσω)	ἐτέλεσα	τετέλεκα	τετέλεσμαι	ἐτελέσθην
τηρέω keep	τηρήσω	ἐτήρησα	τετήρηκα	τετήρημαι	ἐτηρήθην
τίθημι place, put	θήσω	ἔθηκα	τέθεικα	τέθειμαι	ἐτέθην
τιμάω value, honor	τιμήσω	ἐτίμησα	(τετίμηκα)	τετίμημαι	(ἐτιμήθην)
φανερόω make manifest	φανερώσω	ἐφανέρωσα	(πεφανέρωκα)	πεφανέρωμαι	ἐφανερώθην
φιλέω love	(φιλήσω)	ἐφίλησα	πεφίληκα	(πεφίλημαι)	(ἐφιλήθην)
χαίρω rejoice	χαρήσομαι				ἐχάρην

APPENDIX V

FEMININE NOUNS OF THE SECOND DECLENSION

The beginner in Greek learns that, with a very few exceptions, nouns of the second declension ending in -ος are masculine in gender. The exceptions which occur most frequently in the New Testament are ἡ ὁδός and ἡ ἔρημος. Besides these two words, however, there are -- suprisingly enough -- thirty-two additional feminine nouns of the second declension in the New Testament, as well as eighteen other nouns of the second declension which are sometimes masculine and sometimes feminine. Examples of the second group include the words παρθένος and θεός; the former, which is usually feminine, is masculine in Revelation 14:4, and the latter is feminine in Acts 19:37, where it refers to the goddess Artemis (sometimes called Diana).

In several cases what now functions as a noun was originally an adjective of two terminations used with a feminine noun. In the course of time, however, the latter came to be omitted, and the adjective alone was felt to be sufficient. For example, the adjective ἄβυσσος, -ον, means *bottomless*; ἡ ἄβυσσος (supply χώρα, *place*) means *the bottomless place*, hence *the abyss*.

In the following lists the numeral which follows the definition indicates the number of times which that Greek noun appears in the New Testament.

116

A. Feminine Nouns of the Second Declension

ἄβυσσος, -ου, ἡ, the abyss (9)

ἀμέθυστος, -ου, ἡ, an amethyst (1)

ἄμμος, -ου, ἡ, sand (5)

ἄμπελος, -ου, ἡ, a vine (9)

βάσανος, -ου, ἡ, pain, torment (3)

βίβλος, -ου, ἡ, a book (10)

βύσσος, -ου, ἡ, linen (1)

διάλεκτος, -ου, ἡ, a language (6)

διέξοδος, -ου, ἡ, a thoroughfare (1)

δοκός, -οῦ, ἡ, a beam, a log (6)

εἴσοδος, -ου, ἡ, an entrance (5)

ἔξοδος, -ου, ἡ, a departure (3)

ἔρημος, -ου, ἡ, a desert, wilderness (as a substantive, 34)

καλλιέλαιος, -ου, ἡ, a cultivated olive tree (1)

κέδρος, -ου, ἡ a cedar (1)

κιβωτός, -οῦ, ἡ, a box, ark (6)

νάρδος, -ου, ἡ, nard (2)

νῆσος, -ου, ἡ, an island (9)

νόσος, -ου, ἡ, a disease (11)

ὁδός, -οῦ, ἡ, a way, road, journey (102)

παράλιος, -ου, ἡ, a level place (1)

πάροδος, -ου, ἡ, a passing (1)

ῥάβδος, -ου, ἡ a staff, rod (12)

Ῥόδος, -ου, ἡ, (the island of) Rhodes (1)

σάπφειρος, -ου, ἡ, a sapphire (1)

σορός, -οῦ, ἡ, a coffin (1)

σποδός, -οῦ, ἡ, ashes (3)

στάμνος, -ου, ἡ, a jar (1)

συκάμινος, -ου, ἡ, a sycamine tree (1)

τρίβος, -ου, ἡ, a path   (3)

τροφός, -οῦ, ἡ, a nurse   (1)

ὕσσωπος, -ου, ἡ, hyssop   (2)

χαλκολίβανος, -ου, ἡ, burnished bronze   (2)

ψῆφος, -ου, ἡ, a pebble, stone; a vote   (3)

B. Nouns of the Second Declension, Sometimes Masculine,

Sometimes Feminine

ἀλάβαστρος, -ου, ὁ, ἡ, (is also sometimes neuter), an alabaster
    jar   (4)

ἄρκος, -ου, ὁ, ἡ, a bear   (1)

ἄψινθος, -ου, ὁ, ἡ, wormwood   (2)

βάτος, -ου, ὁ, ἡ, a thorn or bramble-bush   (4)

βήρυλλος, -ου, ὁ, ἡ, beryl   (1)

θεός, -οῦ, ὁ, ἡ, God, a god, a goddess   (1323)

θυρωρός, -οῦ, ὁ, ἡ, a doorkeeper, porter, janitor   (4)

κάμηλος, -ου, ὁ, ἡ, a camel   (6)

κάμινος, -ου, ὁ, ἡ, a furnace   (4)

ληνός, -οῦ, ἡ, rarely ὁ, a wine press   (4)

λίβανος, -ου, ὁ, rarely ἡ, frankincense   (2)

λιμός, -οῦ, ὁ, rarely ἡ, hunger, famine   (12)

μάρμαρος, -ου, ὁ, ἡ, marble   (1)

νεωκόρος, -ου, ὁ, ἡ, a temple keeper   (1)

ὄνος, -ου, ὁ, ἡ, an ass   (6)

παρθένος, -ου, ὁ, ἡ, a virgin   (15)

σμάραγδος, -ου, ὁ, ἡ, an emerald   (1)

συγκληρονόμος, -ου, ὁ, ἡ, a fellow heir, joint heir   (4)

ὥσπερ ξένοι χαίρουσι πατρίδα βλέπειν

οὕτως καὶ τοῖς κάμνουσι βιβλίου τέλος